POWER PLAY

To, Dear Paritoshit,

For satisfying your curiosity
about our power problems &
for your reading pleasure—

Pralhush-Varshu
6th May, 2000
Gaithersburg, Md

Power Play
A Study of the Enron Project

Abhay Mehta

Orient Longman

ORIENT LONGMAN LIMITED

Registered Office
3-6-272 Himayatnagar, Hyderabad 500 029 (A.P.), India

Other Offices
Bangalore, Bhubaneshwar, Calcutta, Chandigarh, Chennai, Cochin,
Guwahati, Hyderabad, Jaipur, Lucknow, Mumbai, New Delhi, Patna

© Abhay Mehta, 1999
First Published 2000

ISBN 81 250 1745 3

Typeset by
Scribe Consultants
New Delhi

Printed in India at
Baba Barkha Nath Printers
New Delhi

Published by
Orient Longman Limited
1/24 Asaf Ali Road
New Delhi 110 002

Contents

To,
My Parents

Acknowledgments

A work like this, the epitaph of my involvement in the Enron case, is necessarily indebted to many individuals. The list that follows, by no means exhaustive, is an acknowledgement of the support, often unexpected, that has come my way at various stages and in different ways, both in the course of the litigation and in the subsequent writing.

I acknowledge the primary contribution of Sunip Sen, without whom this enterprise would have stopped before it began; Ragini Sen for her patience and friendship; Shri Shanti Bhushan, who with his incisive and brilliant mind, fought a remarkable battle in the Courts; Prashant Bhushan, for his courage and public spirit, rare in this age; the Bhushan family for their warmth, hospitality and friendship; and Kamini Jaiswal, whose unstinting labour in the case was crucial.

Others whose contribution I wish to acknowledge are Mr Paranjape whose indefatigable energy and sense of purpose defied both circumstances and age, Baburao Samant, P. Kaul and Vivek Monteiro, and in Bangalore, Arun Agrawal (on whose invaluable work a part of chapter 13 rests); Leo Saldahana and Padma Damodaran.

I would like to record my appreciation for the efforts put in by Deepa Hari and Bela Malik for carefully reading and editing my work, to Narayan Rangaraj, Jogesh Motwani, Meena Menon and Vrijendra, whose comments and criticisms have been most helpful in shaping the book.

My thanks to Santosh Menon and Dilip Raote whose initial prodding and encouragement pulled me out of my deep apathy to start work on this book; Thomas Mathew, whose hospitality and support I could take for granted; the late Winin Pereira for the use of his remarkable documentation centre, from which the book draws in several instances; Mangesh Chavan, without whom it would have been physically impossible to go on with the case; my friends, Girish Sant and Santanu Dikshit, to whose work Chapter 10 is largely indebted; Sulabha Brahme and Subash Shah for their invaluable assistance—in matters fiscal and otherwise; Sudha and Murthy whose love and delicious idlis kept me going when I needed it most, Satyendra Rao and Jagruti Dadhia for all their effort in helping me with the corrections; Dhanjibhai of Nisha Xerox for his overnight miracles and long credit lines. Additionally thanks to K. Ashok Rao, Probir Purkayastha, Viswajit Sawant for all their help.

In a different vein, it is my pleasure to acknowledge my gratitude and warmest thanks to Sucheta Dalal, Somshekhar Sunderesan, R.N. Bhaskar, Charubala Annuncio, Sandipan Deb, Sumana Ramanan, Nandu Kulkarni, Praful Bidwai and R. Padmanabhan for restoring my faith in the press. Discussions with them contributed to different parts of the book. Bharat Bhushan's remarkable efforts in investigative journalism laid the foundation for unravelling the story. My thanks to my publishers Orient Longman, India and my editor Hemlata Shankar for taking the book through the editorial process.

This book (as did the litigation) draws on documents that are not a part of the public domain. Individuals, who helped in giving access to documents which are being kept 'top secret'; 'confidential' etc., choose to remain anonymous. I would like to place on record my immense gratitude, as well as their sense of public spirit that prompted them to take the risk. Copies of all documents refered to in the book and xii *Acknowledgments*

others are in the public domain and can be made available on request by emailing the author at am@altindia.net.

Finally, I must state that the conclusions and opinions that have been put forward in the book are my own. I also own full responsibility for any inadvertent errors that may have crept in.

A Chronology of Events

10/91   With the objective of private investment in the power sector, the laws governing various aspects of the electricity sector were extensively amended.

17/6/92   The Enron team's first visit to Bombay.

20/6/92   MoU between Enron and MSEB—the largest contract in Indian history for an admittedly high price and in admitted breach of norms.

8/7/92   The World Bank's Report (solicited by the GoM) states that the project is likely to have adverse financial impact on MSEB.

7/92   The CEA comments on MoU that the price agreed by the MSEB is too high and in breach of prevailing norms.

13/7/92   Enron "advises" the Government of Maharashtra against "auditing" project costs and pre-determining return on equity (both of which are required by law).

4/9/92   Enron's English solicitors set out "The Problems Concerning the Application of the Indian Electricity Act" and solutions that include changing the law and issuing administrative directions.

30/9/92   The Chairman of MSEB, states that public and judicial scrutiny of business policy and decisions as per law not acceptable to a company like DPC.

30/4/93   The World Bank evaluation declares project unviable, because of heavy financial burden on the MSEB along with other matters of concern. Refuses to fund the project.

28/6/93   Enron feels World Bank opinion can be changed, and Indian media can be managed.

26/8/93	Enron asks Maharashtra CM to intercede and influence the CEA, in the discharge of its duties even before Enron begins statutory prerequisites.
8/93	CEA finds the reasonable capital cost of plants, like Enron's to be Rs 1.91 crore per MW (1997 costs). This is against Enron's cost of more than Rs 4 crore/MW.
9/93	In a Cabinet Note, requesting Cabinet of Maharashtra to allow MSEB to sign the PPA, a separate secret note that brings out all negative matters of concern, was left out.
10/9/93	GoM sets an agenda to the GoI: preventing MSEB from exercising its statutory powers, primacy of Enron's tariff structure over the law, restraints from lawful demands for information by any authority from Enron and subverting existing provisions in the Act.
22/9/93	The statutory notification is published by DPC.
3/11/93	FIPB meeting.
10/11/93	DPC replies refusing to supply requested information to CEA.
11/11/93	GoI informs CEA that the cost of power was looked into by the Finance Secretary.
12/11/93	CEA decides not to examine the project.
23/11/93	The Ministry of Power gives a blanket undertaking to the DPC that its application for CEA clearance will be approved.
23/11/93	CEA issues letter stating that the technical aspects of the project are in order and that it cannot examine economic aspects.
6/12/93	MSEB's solicitors clarify that a clearance has not been issued by the CEA.
8/12/93	PPA signed. Only the first phase of 695 MW is binding. MSEB has option not to go ahead with the full project.
5/2/94	Chairman, MSEB requests the GoI to amend the Act or notifications.
10/2/94	State Guarantee signed by the Government of Maharashtra.
24/6/94	State Support Agreement signed between GoM and DPC.
13/7/94	The first litigation against the project filed.

14/7/94   CEA issues another clearance to DPC.

16/9/94   GoI counter-guarantee signed.

8/95   The official Committee of the Government of Maharashtra recommends scrapping the project on several grounds.

8/95   The GoM files a suit against DPC and MSEB in the Bombay High Court seeking cancellation of the PPA on grounds of fraud, corruption and misrepresentation.

7/11/95   Rebecca Mark of Enron meets Bal Thackeray. Misses a scheduled appointment with the Chief Minister of Maharashtra.

8/11/95   GoM in a volte face announces "renegotiations" after its repeated stand that there would be no negotiations and appoints a committee to revive both phases.

19/11/95   The Renegotiation Committee fulfils its mandate and submits its report.

26/1/96   The revival of both phases of the project formally announced by the GoM.

7/3/96   DPC writes to the CEA retaining the tariff of the first phase of the renegotiated project.

22/6/96   The IDBI notes that even after renegotiation, Phase I of the project had not undergone any change.

8/96   The largest contract in the history of India, with contractually binding payments by MSEB to DPC exceeding US $30 billion, (Rs 1,20,000 crore currently) in the form of a binding PPA is signed.

4/97   Supreme Court refuses to entertain an appeal against Enron. Allows appeal against the GoM, petition pending to date (8/99) without any hearing on the matter at all. Work on the project continues as usual.

3/99   Phase 1 of the project on-line.

2001–2   Phase 2 of the project expected to be on-line.

A List of Abbreviations

BJP   The Bharatiya Janata Party

CEA   The Central Electricity authority, a statutory body created under the Electricity (Supply) Act, 1948

DPC   The Dabhol Power Company, Unlimited. A subsidiary registered in India, held by Enron Corp. (8%), Bechtel (10%) and General Electric Corporation (10%). The MSEB may be a 30% partner if it manages to raise the resources

IDBI   The Industrial Development Bank of India

GoI   Government of India

GoM   Government of Maharashtra

LNG   Liquefied Natural Gas

MSEB   The Maharashtra State Electricity Board

MoEF   Ministry of Environment and Forests

MoF   The Ministry of Finance, the Government of India

MoPG   The Ministry of Power, the Government of India

MoU   Memorandum of Understanding

NPV   Net Present Value

PPA   The Power Purchase Agreement; the contract signed between the MSEB and DPC for the supply of about 2000 MW of power and/or capacity from DPC's plant near Dabhol in Maharashtra

Introduction

Over the last five years, private investment in infrastructure development and management has been in the news in one form or another. The power sector in particular has been the focus of much media attention and academic analysis. In the process, a series of myths have sprung up around the sector ranging from power shortages (not that shortages don't exist, but the nature of the shortages remains largely misunderstood) to the belief in the absolute necessity for foreign investment in the power sector.

This book takes up for study the first—and arguably the most controversial—private power project in India. The project has been set up by the Enron Corporation in Maharashtra. The progress of events relating to this project is one of the most interesting chapters in the history of post-independence India. It is an ongoing saga and the last word is yet to be written.

After 1991, the new power policy announced by the Government of India (GoI) allowed for additional private participation in the power sector. Thereafter, in 1993, a contract was signed in Maharashtra between the state owned electricity board (MSEB) and the Indian subsidiary of the

Enron Corporation, the Dabhol Power Company (DPC) for the supply of 695 megawatts (MW) of electricity.

The contract between the two parties was signed after detailed examinations of various aspects of the project were conducted by both the central and state governments. It was claimed that all necessary clearances required by law were obtained. In particular, the 'techno-economic' clearance was purportedly issued after an examination of the technical and economic aspects of the project by the sole authority under the law, the Central Electricity Authority (CEA).

While this was going on, there was a great deal of opposition to the project on various ideological, economic, political and environmental grounds. The opposition came from the most diverse quarters. These included political parties, a loose knit coalition of former chairmen of the CEA and various state electricity boards, environmentalists, consumer organisations, academics, the World Bank, and so on.

The contract also proved to be politically controversial in the state of Maharashtra. Most of the parties in the opposition including the Shiv Sena and the Bharatiya Janata Party (BJP) opposed the project for a number of reasons. In the elections that followed, an alliance of the Shiv Sena and the BJP came to power in April 1995, almost solely on the issue of possible malfeasance in the contract. The new government undertook to re-examine the terms and conditions of the contract.

After a detailed examination by a special cabinet committee, the Government of Maharashtra (GoM) came to a conclusion, inter alia, that the contract was not in the public interest. It decided to cancel the contract in August 1995.

To legally substantiate that decision, the GoM filed a suit in the Bombay High Court. This suit sought the cancellation of the contract. A compendious number of documents from the records of the GoM were attached to substantiate the various allegations in the suit.

Within three months of that decision, for reasons that are still not fully clear, the government backtracked on its decision without assigning any reasons.

It went on to 'renegotiate' the contract without any change in the old contract.

Following the 'renegotiated' agreement by the GoM, the other parties involved in the whole issue—the MSEB and DPC signed an agreement in August 1996 for the supply of about 2000 MW of electricity to the MSEB in the form of available capacity and gas for a period of twenty years.

The payments due on the renegotiated contract constitute one of the largest contracts (civilian or military) in world history, and the single largest contract in this country's history. Payments amount to about US$ 1300 million in the first year of Phase 2 of the project going online. Total payments amount to about US$ 35,000 million (Rs 1,25,000 crore) over the life of the contract. The payments are linked to various indices including, among others, the oil-price index, making exact estimation completely contingent on an assumption of the rate of change in various indices. In any case, a conservative low-end estimate of the net present value (NPV) of this stream of payments is about US$ 17 billion (Rs 70,000 crore) to about US$23 to 25 billion (Rs 1,00,000 to Rs 1,06,000 crore) at the middle end.

The terms for the purchase of electricity by a utility are also unprecedented in the country's history. The purchase of electricity by the MSEB and the payments due therein are governed by various agreements signed. These agreements include the PPA (Power Purchase Agreement), the Guarantee by the state of Maharashtra, the State Support Agreement, the Counter Guarantee by the Union of India and the tripartite agreement between the GoM, the GoI and the Reserve Bank of India.

These terms include a guarantee from the GoM that in case of default in payments by the MSEB, the state of Maharashtra would be liable for all and any payments due to the DPC by the MSEB under the terms of the contract. The state government has put a lien on all its assets: past, present and future in this respect. The interpretation of the state guarantee is through the application of English law in exclusion to Indian law.

The Republic of India, has in turn counter-guaranteed the payments due to the DPC. In case the GoM defaults in its guarantee, the Government of India is liable for payments upto 1500 crores a year (indexed to inflation, the dollar, etc.). The GoI will directly deduct from the constitutionally sanctioned share of revenues due to the state of Maharashtra in case of the GoI having to make any payments. The Republic of India too has staked all its assets (including those abroad, save diplomatic and military) as surety for the payments due to the DPC by the MSEB.

Additionally, the terms include the *de facto* import of nearly everything including the equipment and the fuel, no transfer of technology, and payments more or less totally in foreign exchange.

This book examines these aspects in some detail. The chapters are set out in chronological order. The first chapter is a 'primer' on Electricity. Chapters 2 to 7 detail the early history of the project. In particular they examine the role of various statutory and constitutional institutions in clearing a way for the project. Chapters 8 to 12 chronicles both the opposition to the project (legal, environmental, technical, economic and political) and examines the nature of the agreements that have been signed. The cancellation of the project consequent to the various objections and the subsequent renegotiations over the project form the penultimate chapters.

Appendix 1 is an examination of another deal that took place at around the same time—the transfer of the

Mukta-Panna oilfields to a consortium of Reliance Industries and Enron.

The narrative in this study is factual and chronological. It is based on internal official government correspondence, files and documentation largely marked 'Secret' or 'Confidential'. Correspondence, internal notes, minutes of meetings etc. from sources as diverse as notes prepared for the cabinets of India as well as Maharashtra; the Prime Minister's Office (PMO), the Foreign Investment Promotion Board (FIPB), the Ministry of Finance (MoF), the Ministry of Power (MoP), the Ministry of Petroleum and Natural Gas (MoPG) and the CEA at the Centre and in Maharashtra, the GoM's and MSEB's internal documentation form the basis of this book. All of these are in the author's possession and can be made available.

1

A Primer on Electricity

Electricity is one of the most ubiquitous commodities that surround us. However, unlike other commodities, it has to be necessarily consumed when produced. It cannot be stored except in another form and its conversion of electricity to another form results in a loss of energy.

Almost all the electricity in the world is produced by burning fossil fuels (coal, natural gas and fractions from the distillation of crude oil). Technically, the production process is quite simple. Fuel is burnt, the burning fuel produces and/or heats gases which then drive turbines. These rotate, producing electricity. The efficiency of the process depends primarily on the fuel used. It ranges from 30–40 per cent in the case of coal and about 46–54 per cent in the case of gas.

To illustrate this process, consider a kilogram (kg) of good quality Indian coal. In theory, if all the energy in the coal were converted to electricity, it would produce about 3.5 units of electricity. However, only 1.25 units of electricity are produced in a typical power station at an efficiency of about 35 per cent.[1] This electricity is then transported across

---

[1] In the most advanced power stations using coal, the efficiency is of

distances, so some of it is necessarily lost. This loss ('transmission loss') ranges between 1 per cent to 7 per cent.[2] The electricity is then used by the consumer. The process of consumption leads to further losses (between 50 to 90 per cent, depending on the efficiency of the device). For example, as much as 80 per cent of the electricity that reaches a typical incandescent bulb is lost in the form of heat.

This means that the overall conversion efficiency from coal to a light bulb in the house is of the order of 7.5 per cent. A typical urban middle-class household consuming 250 units a month[3] uses about 8 kg of coal a day or 2.4 tonnes of coal a year.[4]

The production and distribution of electricity are simple enough. The difficulty lies in the choice of technologies and the series of conscious choices that a society makes (or does not choose to make). These conscious choices range from the choice of production techniques to environmental issues. It is to be appreciated that these are choices undertaken with conscious intent for most parts.

Consider a few of these choices. About 80 per cent of the

---

the order 40–42 per cent. Similarly, the efficiency of a gas based station ranges from about 35 per cent in a simple cycle station. With secondary heat recovery processes installed, (a combined cycle plant) the efficiency is about 10 per cent more with standard production technology and as much as 20 per cent more with state of the art technology i.e. the efficiency reaches as much as 55 per cent.

[2]The loss of power during transmission is proportional to the distance, the equipment used, the transformers at the other end, the step up voltage and the kind of conductor used (copper versus aluminum).

[3]A boiler, six to seven bulbs, one or two tube lights, a TV, a refrigerator and some appliances (washing machine/iron etc.).

[4]Interestingly enough, an additional 0.8–1.2 tonnes of coal equivalent is used by average middle class households in the form of cooking gas. The total coal equivalent used in a household amounts to as much as three and a half tonnes a year.

electricity produced in India today comes from coal. Coal is quite cheap and available in large quantities.[5] Singrauli, a region in Bihar, produces enough coal to illuminate a large part of India, but leaves most of its inhabitants without electricity. The living and working conditions of the town residents are among the worst in the country.

Another of these choices is illustrated by the problem of ash. Burning coal leaves a considerable amount of residual ash. The quantity of ash generated in India amounts to about seventy million tonnes a year. This ash can be used in a number of ways ranging from a base for building materials such as bricks, road foundations, etc. However, for most parts, there is no further use made of the ash and it is simply dumped in a huge hole (known as the ash pond). For an average power station, the ash pond itself amounts to a few hundred acres. To date, there has been no conscious decision to use these mountains of ash constructively or to enforce any such action.

Air pollution and its abatement is yet another example. Burning coal spews a large number of gases, chiefly oxides of nitrogen (NO_x: i.e. NO_2 and NO), sulphur dioxide (SO_2) and carbon dioxide (CO_2). The amount of SO_2 and NO_x can be reduced very considerably, as much as 85 to 90 per cent, by a variety of standard techniques. The investment required to install state-of-the-art pollution reduction devices amounts to an additional 20 per cent or so over the cost of the generating equipment. This additional 20 per cent means an additional 5 paise a unit of electricity. However, most power generating stations in India are equipped with only rudimentary pollution control equipment. The new ones coming up, save a few, are no better.

---

[5]Albeit only in a few locations in the country.

The Crisis of the System

The mass scale production of power began after independence with an annual growth rate of about seven to eight per cent per annum (p.a.). The power system is, as most systems in India inherited from colonial times are, in a state of perpetual crisis, lurching from bad to worse.

The symptoms are obvious to anyone outside of Bombay: regular power cuts ranging from an hour to most of the day, irregular supply, and voltage fluctuations for those lucky enough to receive power in the first place.

The reasons for this state of affairs are myriad. We have one of the highest rates of 'transmission and distribution losses' (T&D losses) in the world,[6] one of the world's lowest utilisations of installed capacity and a host of other problems. Official estimates of T&D losses in the country range from 10 per cent to as much as 60 per cent. These official estimates are highly unreliable and in most cases very low. In Maharashtra, the official rate is claimed to be 15.7 per cent, which is among the lowest in the country. However, since nearly 40 per cent of the total generation of electricity in Maharashtra is supplied without any metering, it is quite likely that the real losses are much higher than the official figure. A realistic estimate of Maharashtra's T&D losses would probably be around 30 per cent.

Most of these T&D losses are simply a euphemism for theft. Power is very easy to steal. A magnet over the meter, disconnecting the meter altogether, or a brick connected to a conducting wire thrown over a transmission line, and of

---

[6]The network in India is widely dispersed at the distribution end. The rate of loss at the distribution end in India is one of the highest in the world if one were to go by any official number whatsoever. The losses range from 15.85% officially in Maharashtra (an untrue figure, it probably amounts to about 27–30%) to 44% in Orissa (this jumped up from 23% to 44% after corporatization).

course, paying the linesman are standard ways. A slightly more sophisticated way is to mount up huge bills that are then written off. The Mula Pravara Cooperative Society owes the MSEB about Rs 250 crore. The scion of the cooperative society defected to the Shiv Sena and was awarded a ministerial post. No action has been taken to date on the outstanding dues (the overdue payments start from a decade ago). MSEB accounts for these as 'receivables' and simply writes off a fraction each year as bad debts.

Delhi is the worst and represents the future of India in many respects. The rate of T&D losses in Delhi is an alarming 60 per cent, representing a theft rate of nearly 54 per cent. Out of every 100 units received/produced by the board, over half, simply disappears. In no other city of the world is such theft tolerated. DESU (Delhi Electricity Supply Undertaking) is one of the most corrupt and bankrupt organisations in the country. The middle class and the industries account for anything between 60–80 per cent of the theft. Contrary to popular assumption, a relatively small part of the theft is by 'jhuggi' (slum) dwellers.[7] For example, almost none of the buildings in East Delhi have regular meters. Even affluent upper middle class and elite housing societies that are over a decade old do not possess a 'regular' meter. Instead, most households receive a fixed (and absurdly low) bill that is totally incommensurate with the actual consumption of electricity.

Bombay presents a striking contrast to Delhi. Bombay has a unique mixture of a private sector organisation (BSES)

---

[7]Not that they don't steal, but the theft of electricity is relatively small, at best a bulb or two, perhaps a fan and a TV. Middle and upper class households with air conditioners, water boilers, irons, etc. need 30 to 40 times the amount of electricity. For example, older air conditioners use about 2 kW of electricity an hour, i.e. the electricity used by an air conditioner is equivalent to that of thirty five 60 W bulbs.

serving the suburbs and a public sector organisation (the BEST) serving the city. The average rate of T&D losses for both organisations is the lowest in the country. It is roughly the same for both BEST and BSES (about 11%). Both are extremely profitable entities: BEST's profits cross-subsiding its transport division and BSES is a favourite on the bourses.

The Demand for Power

The installed capacity in India as of 1996 is 84,000 MW.[8] The peak demand is at best of the order of 60,000 MW, perhaps less. On the face of it there should be a surplus of power. But obviously that is not the case.

The demand for power varies drastically at various times in the day. There is a sudden surge in demand in the morning, as middle class consumers switch on their boilers and other appliances. This surge is repeated in the evening when nearly everyone turns on their lights at the same time. The maximum demand is known as the peak demand. At night, the demand is considerably lower, in fact almost less than half the peak demand.

India's shortages are largely peak shortages. At this stage, a look into the system itself may be useful. As stated earlier power cannot be stored. Therefore, the system must be ready at all times to meet the changing pattern of demand. The installed capacity has to be more than the peak demand to be able to meet it.

For various reasons set out here the peak demand is not fulfilled, resulting in a serious shortage of power. The prime factor is the availability of power stations (i.e. the average time that a power station is actually capable of generating power). Most power stations in India run on coal. The coal is not

---

[8]One of the most difficult numbers to come by, is the figure for the total installed capacity in the country. Most official sources, have *stopped* giving this figure for the last five years. The number used has been gleaned from a large variety of official sources.

delivered to them on time either because of a failure to pay (as in the case of Delhi and other boards) or due to the unavailability of wagons.

The State Electricity Boards (SEBs) owed the National Thermal Power Corporation (NTPC) Rs 6,500 crore in October 1997, i.e. more than 60 per cent of NTPC's turnover. NTPC in turn is unable to pay Coal India (CIL) and other suppliers of fuel. The total outstandings of all the SEBs to various suppliers (NTPC, CIL, the railways, etc.) totalled Rs 18,500 crore at the end of October 1998.[9] The boards themselves do not have the money for a variety of reasons, largely because of large scale theft and fiscal mismanagement.

Power stations are located at some distance from the mines and enormous quantities of coal have to be transported to them. For the usual set of reasons, the number of wagons available to the railways and their turnaround time is relatively low. Therefore the coal does not reach the stations on time. Depletion of stocks leads to a shutdown. A thermal power station requires about a fortnight to be turned on again.

A large fraction (a quarter or about 20,000 MW) of the stations in India are over twenty-five years old. Besides age, the problems of poor or indifferent maintenance lead to regular breakdown in equipment. The resulting shutdowns are euphemistically attributed to 'unscheduled maintenance' as opposed to planned shutdowns for planned maintenance and repairs.

All these problems which can be resolved easily, reduce the availability of power stations. It ranges from a low of 40 to 50 per cent in Bihar, a moderate 80 per cent in Maharashtra to a high of 90 per cent and above in the case of NTPC. What the numbers mean, say at an average availability of 75 per cent, is that over the course of a year, the station is

---

[9]As reported in the *Hindu* of 18 December, 1998.

incapable of producing power for 25 per cent of that time, i.e. 91 days of the year.

The low availability is further exacerbated by the pattern of demand for electricity in India. The effective utilisation of installed capacity is one of the lowest in the world. Even with an installed capacity of 84,000 MW, it is not possible to meet the peak demand of 60,000 MW since the actual production is considerably lower (about 45,000 MW), leading to massive shortages.

The Cost of Power

The cost of power comprises the cost of generation and the cost of distribution. The cost of generation in turn comprises the cost of fuel and the expenses of setting up the plant which consists of turbines, incinerators, secondary heat recovery devices and pollution abatement devices.

The generation of electricity is a capital intensive and technologically demanding industry. Only six companies in the world produce power generating equipment. The price of equipment (in US$ terms) has shown only notional (in the range of 2% p.a.) increases over the last twenty years. This is despite several substantial technological improvements.[10]

The main reason is the over capacity of production together with the low increase in demand. The demand for electricity in the West has reached historic lows since the late seventies onwards due to various reasons. The oil price crises and the resulting increase in efficiencies mandated by government in every aspect of the economy, together with the shift in the pattern of industrial growth from the so called

---

[10]The average efficiency of gas turbines has increased from 30% in open cycle operations to about 54% (proven and in commercial operations) in the case of combined cycle turbines. A claim of 60% efficiency has been made by ABB among others, but these are not yet in commercial operation.

smoke stack and energy intensive industries (iron, steel etc.) to the so called sunshine industries (information, service industries and the rest), have resulted in a drop in the rate of increase of demand for electricity from an average of 10–12 per cent in the fifties to 7–8 per cent in the sixties, and further slowed down to 2–3 per cent in the late seventies and early eighties. Some examples to include federally mandated increases in efficiencies in the car industry, the refrigerator industry and others in the USA. The Japanese pattern is even more relevant. There has been a growth in GDP without a corresponding growth in energy demand, in fact, the demand for energy has declined as a result of increased efficiencies.

For a combined cycle plant of very high efficiencies, the average installed cost of the power station[11] is of the order of US $400/kWh or Rs 1.6 crore/MW (in current rupees). The cost of equipment amounts to less than half of that, i.e., US $200/kWh or Rs 0.8 crore/MW. It is to be noted that this is true even of Enron. The official cost of the equipment is about 1 crore a MW[12] out of a total cost of Rs 4.5 crore a MW. Coal stations are somewhat more expensive (about 20 to 30%), but compensate by much lower fuel costs.

Coal costs about 50 to 70 paisa/unit while gas costs about Rs 1.40 a unit (1997 prices). Liquid fuel is the most expensive fuel, amounting to about Rs 2 per unit of electricity.

The prices of equipment in India follow an interesting curve. With this figure of US $400 a kW as a benchmark, the price of setting up a power station in India, ought to have followed a similar trend, increasing only with the devaluation of the rupee and the higher rates of interest in India i.e. about US $450/kW (Rs 1.8 crore a MW) in the case of a gas station and about US $500/kW (Rs 2 crore a MW) to US $550/kW (Rs 2.2 crore a MW) for a coal station.

---

[11]This includes interest during construction (IDC) and other costs.

[12]The IDBI appraisal report on the Enron project.

In the late seventies nearly all international tenders floated in India for power equipment were won by Bharat Heavy Electricals Ltd. (BHEL)[13] at prices equivalent to, or in fact, slightly cheaper than those prevailing in the West. The massive expansion of NTPC beginning in the early eighties set a trend for prices in India being slightly (10 to 12%) higher than one would expect.

The Jain hawala papers reveal that nearly half the officials who received money from them were officials from the power sector. These payments were for the selection of equipment on a one time basis on the lines of the defence contracts.

In the case of Bofors, the money was paid as a "commission" for selecting the guns. This "commission" (Rs 150 crore then) amounted to about 10 per cent of the value of the guns (Rs 1500 crore then). The guns were by all accounts, if not the best in the fudged tests, among the top three in different tests. The difference between the competing guns was not of that order of magnitude as in the case of, say, a luxury car as compared to a modest family car, but between similar products differing notionally.

The case of power generating equipment was somewhat similar till 1992. Officials of various public sector enterprises were offered commissions for the purchase of specific equipment. There was a difference of around seven to eight per cent in the prices of comparable equipments as compared to international or local prices.

This continued to be the position of the import of equipment for indigenously run and maintained power stations until 1992, after which there was a sea change.

---

[13]India is one of the few countries in the world that can manage to produce its own power generating equipment to a large extent. This is the case because of a conscious decision by the state.

2

The Events of 1991

The events of 1991 proved to be a watershed for India. The country was plunged into a deep financial crisis brought about by profligate spending, particularly on defence imports, dwindling reserves of foreign exchange and the flight of capital from the country. The Narasimha Rao government was forced to adopt a substantial change in course. It can perhaps be argued that the policies adopted were, in more than one sense, simply a continuation of the previous government's policies, particularly that of V.P. Singh's. After two or three years of token opposition from both the left and the right, a national consensus on this issue seems to have evolved.

Capital Crisis and Foreign Capital

The entry of foreign private capital in power, petroleum, and telecom was a welcome, radical change and, in fact unprecedented. In other sectors, particularly consumer goods, a case can be made that, barring the easing of barriers precluding direct entry, the apparent shift was really a continuum.

The entry of foreign capital in countries across the globe

is illustrated in the financial markets. The eighties saw the largest transfer of capital from the developed to the developing countries, particularly in terms of the institutional money targeted at emerging markets. Between 1991 and 1996 for example, American institutions invested about US $400 billion in emerging markets. The sum total of American investment in the Indian stock markets is not even a fraction of that number, in this case of the order of one per cent or less.

The official line was that the barriers against the entry of foreign private capital were lifted in order to augment available resources in the face of a resource crunch. Crucial were the conditionalities attached to the loans that the country had taken from the World Bank (WB) to stave off the crisis of 1991. The covenants and conditions of specific loan agreements demanded the introduction of private capital in specific sectors like the petroleum sector.[14] However, it needs to be noted that in other sectors, particularly the power sector, there was no explicit compulsion from the WB, short of the usual homilies, to introduce private capital, but the change in policy in the power sector had been already planned by the Indian government.[15]

In May/June 1992, a team of the Government of India[16] toured the USA with the aim of inviting producers of power in the USA to invest in India. Pursuant to its policy of inviting private sector participation, the government drew up a list of projects in which the private sector could participate. Most of these were coal based stations for which preliminary spade work had been done. There were two or three gas based projects also in the list. Among others, the Enron Corporation in particular, showed a 'keen interest' in setting-up a power

---

[14]See the introduction in Appendix 1.

[15]See Chapter 3.

[16]The high level team of the government comprised of the cabinet secretary, the secretaries of power and finance.

station in India based on the import of liquefied natural gas (LNG).

Enron's Corporate Profile

It has been claimed on numerous occasions that Enron is among the "world's leading power companies". This was stated on oath to the courts as well as in innumerable press reports and all official governmental correspondence.

Enron is primarily a gas distribution company. It figures in the list of the 500 largest corporations in the USA.

In 1993, the total sales of Enron were US$7.1 billion (22,000 crore).[17] Of this, only 1 per cent[18] [$73 million or Rs 220 crore at that time] of their total revenues was derived from electricity. In contrast, almost all Indian power companies, private or state-owned had sales higher than that. When the company first came to India, its experience in building and running power stations was limited to a few stations in the US and the Philippines, of capacities ranging from 28, 105 and 110 MW stations in the Philippines, and a 110 MW station in Puerto Rico, to 149 MW to 450 MW plants in the USA.[19]

The Memorandum of Understanding (MoU)

In India, the company proposed to set up a mega power generating station to be run on gas. This gas would be imported and brought to India in the form of liquefied natural gas (LNG). The size of the proposed station was about 2500 MW that would consume the output of an entire train of LNG.

---

[17]Annual Report of Enron Corporation for 1993.
[18]*Ibid.*
[19]*Ibid.*

In most parts of the world natural gas is simply transported through a pipeline. Gas that comes out of a field has three primary fractions—a fraction of the gas that cannot be liquefied, a fraction that can be liquefied very easily by merely applying pressure to it and a fraction which is liquefiable only under extraordinary conditions of extremely cold temperatures of −165°C. Liquefied natural gas is natural gas liquefied under these extraordinary conditions of temperature and pressure. LNG can be transported across distances since the degree of compression is of the order of over a thousand fold.

Unlike most petroleum products, LNG is not amenable to spot purchases. It is not a tradable commodity and there is no market in LNG. The process of liquefying natural gas requires a capital investment of the order of US $4 billion at the liquefaction end. Additionally, the transportation requires specially constructed refrigerated ships capable of maintaining the gas at low temperatures. Each ship involves an investment of US$150 to US$200 million. A fleet of four to six ships is required. The overall capital requirements are of the order of US$5 billion. Furthermore, at the receiving end, specialised terminals (regassification terminals) are needed to convert the liquefied product back to gas.

Given the extraordinary capital investment, the only way a producer would invest the necessary capital, is if there were a long-term contract signed with a purchaser. A typical contract for the supply of LNG is of the order of US$15 billion. The amounts are so enormous, given the capital recovery of US$5 billion and the base price of gas. Each such deal is unique.

Given its geographical location and near total lack of petroleum resources, Japan is the main importer of LNG. Unlike us, it manages to import large quantities at prices that are cheaper than the oil equivalent. Optimum use is made by having the LNG regassification terminal near warehouses that are used for the storage of frozen imported food to utilise the extremely low temperatures. Conversely, given the economics of LNG, power stations of about 2400 MW are needed to consume the gas from a single supply train.

On 15 June 1992, a team of officials from Enron Corporation and General Electric Company (GE) arrived in New Delhi. They held discussions with the chairman of the ONGC and the Petroleum Secretary. The team arrived in Bombay on the evening of 17 June. On 18 and 19 June, 1992, the team visited over half a dozen potential sites in Maharashtra, and on the morning of 20 June the MSEB was "handed a term sheet" by the team.

Thereafter, on the same day, the MSEB signed a Memorandum of Understanding (MoU) with Enron and GE. This MoU specified that the MSEB would buy electricity and/or capacity from Enron which would build, own, and operate (but not transfer) a plant of about 2000–2400 MW (nominal) capacity. The power station was to be built near Dabhol in the Ratnagiri district, about 300 km south of Bombay. The MoU was signed within three days of Enron's arrival in Bombay. The MoU specified that a plant "with a minimum capacity of 2000 MW" would be set up, that the MSEB "agreed" to the "need to set up a 2000 MW plant" to be "run on liquefied natural gas (LNG)", that the "electrical power purchase contract" would be a "contract for 20 years term between power venture and MSEB", and that the "Contract (was) to be structured to achieve an all in all price of US \$0.073/kWh (Rs 2.34 per unit at the then prevailing exchange rates)."[20]

An electricity generating plant plant is usually set up after an initial examination of the context in which the plant is to be used is determined and the need and pattern of demand for electricity are assesed. Maharashtra, like the rest of India, suffers from a peaking shortage. Then there are enormous reserves of one of the world's best qualities of coal at

---

[20]MoU dated 20.6.93 signed by the MSEB with Enron Development Corporation. This like all documents that are to be used in this narrative is a secret document.

Chandrapur in Maharashtra. In the light of this background, the MoU between Enron and the MSEB posed a problem. The MoU had already specified the size of the plant, the fact that imported fuel (about 4 times as expensive as the best quality of coal) was to be used and the final price that was to be paid to Enron for the electricity. The MoU foreclosed, among other things, the question and impact of pricing, questions and analyses of Maharashtra's needs (peaking versus baseload), the relative economics of coal versus imported natural gas, the forex considerations, the meta economics, pricing, inviting other parties to quote a price and so on. The list is endless.

At the prices they had quoted for a unit, for the total capacity of 2000 MW the MSEB would be paying a sum in the region of US $1300 million every year (about Rs 400 crores). Over the life of the contract, the total payments would be in the region of thirty five billion US dollars. Such a contract, would be the single largest purchase contract in the history of this country.

There is no explanation on record or otherwise as to why a decision that involved the largest series of payments in India's history was taken so quickly. None of these issues, for a completely mysterious set of reasons, appear to have been considered at all.

3

The Review of a Fait Accompli

The signing of the MoU between Enron and the MSEB represents an extraordinary deviation from all established convention in similar cases the world over. First, the examination of the terms and conditions and implications of the project followed the events. Contrary to existing legal provisions, economic rationale and sheer common sense, the nation was presented with a fait accompli.

The law, elementary economics, as well as plain common sense dictate that there be an examination of the basic parameters underlying a power plant. Among the parameters that need to be examined are the capital cost of the plant (on which the price of electricity depends), the fuel, the location of the plant, the type of fuel, etc. In India the law mandated that this examination would be done by an autonomous organisation, the CEA (Central Electricity Authority).

The International Framework of Laws

Given the inherently monopolistic nature of the electricity

business, particularly at the distribution end, every country mandates the operation of all such entities within a framework of laws. The laws governing public utilities across the world regulate the operational and financial aspects of utility operations. Generally, even the most trivial aspect of the operation of utilities is regulated. The price, is especially, rigorously governed by stringent regulations and is the subject of great scrutiny: administrative; judicial; quasi-judicial and of course public. This is 'normal' in any utility or independent generator the world over.

These laws impose a cap on the amount of profits that can be made. In the USA, the stock of electric utilities are what is termed as 'widow and orphan' stocks, i.e., safe, with more or less guaranteed returns. However, at the same time the statutory control and explicit limitations on profits ensure that the value of these stocks will not change much over time.

With the neo-conservative shift in the US and the wave of privatisation in Britain in the late seventies and early eighties the industry was deregulated to some extent. Competition to supply electricity to utility companies was permitted. It is important to understand that the supply of electricity to a distributor is amenable to competition but the very nature of electricity and the amount of capital investment dictate that the distribution of electricity remains in one hand, whether it is public or private.[21]

---

[21]In the current milieu in India today, it is not uncommon to find otherwise well-informed citizens or even officials, advocating the introduction of competition in distribution. This is simply not feasible in purely economic terms at the retail level to individual consumers. There is no country in the world where this has been done nor will it be contemplated in the near term at the currently prevailing and immediately foreseeable levels of technology.

The Policy or the Lack thereof in India

At the outset, it needs to be stated that India is probably the only country in the world that did *not* (and to date i.e., 1999, does not) have a power policy. This is despite the law (the Electricity Supply Act) that specifically (enacted in 1948 to premote a "national power policy") such a policy at the national level. There has been no attempt to do so, despite constant crises. At best, the attempt has been to issue directions (and not policy *per se*) on a 'need to' basis or lately on a case by case basis. The case by case basis is perhaps to be taken literally. The government, of course, has given no reasons to explain why it has failed to do so, considering that fifty years have elapsed since it was supposed to, and in the light of the fact that it is under a specific statutory obligation to do so. The changes in this sector have all been ad hoc. The inadequacy and the complete failure of the system can be attributed to this.

Until 1991, the role of the private sector in the power sector was marginal. The few existing private companies had been operational even before Independence. The role for new participants, although not explicitly restricted by law, was extremely limited. In 1991, the law was amended to allow for increased private sector participation. Private players were invited to set up plants for the generation of electricity.

The law mandated a specific set of generous terms by which electricity from these plants could be then sold to the state electricity boards. Private parties were told that they could sell the electricity on a cost-plus basis, i.e., after accounting for all costs and a reasonable rate of return. A 16 per cent return on the equity investment was assured by law.

The Electricity (Supply) Act, 1948 (ESA) was amended. As amended the act specified a particular procedure for proposals involving more than a certain capital expenditure (25 crores then). The generating company had to prepare a scheme which included revenue details (and therefore tariffs), its financing agreements, the costing of the projects, the need for extra electricity supply and the generation estimate, among other things. Before finalising the scheme and submitting it to the Central Electricity Authority (CEA), the proposed scheme was to be notified and advertised to the public. The public is allowed to make representations to the company. The statute allowed a period of two months for such representations. The Act specifically provides that the scheme can be submitted to the CEA only after this period of two months and after considering all representations and if necessary modifying the scheme after considering the representations.

The CEA then evaluates the scheme, checking that the scheme provides for reasonable capital expenditure (i.e. the promoters do not inflate capital expenditures since this would increase the tariff of electricity and, of course, the profits to the company). The CEA is bound by the statue to verify if the estimates of prospective supply of electricity and the revenue from its sales are reasonable. Additionally, the CEA is required to approve the capital costs and the financial package. The reasonableness of expenditure on revenue and the capital account is the critical part of the CEA's duty and is the only real safeguard provided to the consumer by the law. After concurrence, if any, by the CEA, the generating company is required to again notify and advertise the entire scheme.

Further, a generating company can enter into a contract only to sell the electricity that it actually generates and not its generating capacity. Section 43-A states that the tariff for the sale of electricity by a State Electricity Board or a generating company will automatically be determined in accordance with the norms of operation and plant load factor (PLF) as laid down by the CEA and the rates of depreciation and reasonable return and other factors as laid down by the

Indian government. This section is mandatory, there could be no deviations from the norms that had been set.

Other important features of the CEA's original notification of 31 March 1992 include the plant load factor which was set, for normal operation, in the range of 68.5 per cent. This level of PLF ensured the full recovery of fixed costs. Additional incentive payment for generation, presumably if required by the board, above that level would be at the negotiated rates.

The entire tariff was to be based on capital costs which had been approved by the CEA in its techno-economic clearance (Section 29–31 of the ESA). The tariff was to be fixed for a period of five years. All elements of interest on loan capital claimed were to be computed on the basis of an "approved financial package" (i.e. the total amount of debt, the rates of interest and the repayment schedule of loans) as approved in the techno-economic clearance. Return on equity was defined as return on the equity of the generating company relevant to the generating unit, with a maximum return of 16 per cent. Equity related to peripheral matters, e.g., ports and harbour costs, airstrips, etc., would not be considered equity for the purpose of the return and could not be cleared as fixed costs.

To summarise, the primary factors determining the sale price of power to the SEB are the capital cost of the project and the financial package. A critical examination and approval by the CEA of these factors is therefore mandated by the Act. An honest and fair examination by the CEA was and is the only protection granted to the public under the law. These regulations are in fact substantially less onerous than say in the US.[22]

---

[22]The Delaware regulations run into 38,000 words or nearly three quarter the size of the book. These and others are available with the author and were provided by Prayas. Extracts from a single section are quoted here: (*contd*)

The CEA's Analysis of the MoU

In July 1992, the CEA analysed the MoU. It was unequivocal in its comments and pointed out that the price of power agreed on was a "departure from the existing norms and parameters notified by the Government"—it was against the existing law which had been specifically modified just eight months earlier to allow private sector participation. It went on to say that "denominating the price in US dollars" was "also a departure from the existing norms".

(*contd.*) (3) "Rate base" means:

(a) The original cost of all used and useful utility plant and intangible assets either to the first person who committed said plant or assets to public use or, at the option of the Commission, the first recorded book cost of said plant or assets; *less*

(b) Related accumulated depreciation and amortization; *less*

(c) The actual amount received and unrefunded as customer advances or contributions in aid of construction of utility plant, and *less*

(d) Any accumulated deferred and unamortized income taxes and investment credits related to plant included in paragraph (a) above, *plus*

(e) Accumulated depreciation of customer advances and contributions in aid of construction related to plant included in paragraph (a) above, *plus*

(f) Materials and supplies necessary to the conduct of the business and investor supplied cash working capital, and *plus*

(g) Any other element of property which, in the judgment of the Commission, is necessary to the effective operation of the utility.

— Rate Base is dollar value of utility's plant employed in providing its service to the public and upon which the utility and its investors are entitled to earn a fair return.

— Rate of return is percentage figure set by Commission. This percentage is multiplied against the rate base in order to determine a fair return to the utility.

— Fair return to utility is amount sufficient to pay operating expenses, to attract new investors, and to pay a fair return to the utility's existing investors.

— The dollar figure representing a fair return to the utility is the product of the rate base of the utility applied to the utility's rate of return, plus the utitlity's operating expenses.

The CEA found that the price that had been agreed upon, i.e. US$0.073/kWh (Rs 2.19 at the then rate of exchange, Rs 3.14 at current rates of exchange) was "considered high". It needs to be kept in mind that even a one-paisa difference in tariffs involves payments of Rs 17 crore a year for a project this size. The CEA went on to state that "the entire MoU" was "one sided".

Given the 'cost plus' approach mandated by the law and the guaranteed 16 per cent return on equity, an examination of the stated cost of the project was crucial. Until the arrival of Enron, the average cost of a CCGT project was in the range of Rs 1.8 crore a MW. This particular project involved additional costs like a jetty, a port, and regassification and storage facilities. These amounted to about Rs 1200 crore even as per Enron's own reckoning. However, the actual cost of the project, as acknowledged by Enron was considerably higher, by over 70 per cent.

The World Bank's Analysis of the MoU

The MSEB did not carry out an internal examination of the MoU or it is unavailable. But the MoU was also submitted to the World Bank for evaluation. On 8 July 1992, The World Bank wrote to the GoM and the MSEB stating,

> "...this large project which is nearly 20 per cent of its (MSEB's) installed capacity, is likely to have an adverse financial impact...(on MSEB)..."

Examining the Project

While it was clear that the cost of the project and the cost of power from the project needed to be examined, other equally important aspects also required scrutiny. These included the forex component, the need for a base-load capacity of this magnitude particularly in the light of the accepted need for peaking power, and whether this project fitted the criterion of being the 'most economical'. The very viability of the MSEB system was not examined by Indian authorities.

The total sales of MSEB in 1992 amounted to about Rs 4400 crore. The installed capacity available for Maharashtra is nearly 11,582 MW. MSEB's own capacity totals 7762 MW. The additional capacity provided by Enron amounts to a 18 per cent increase in Maharashtra installed capacity. For this 18 per cent rise in capacity, the MSEB set aside nearly all its revenues to be able to pay Enron.

The situation was much the same six years later. After unprecedented rise in electricity prices in Maharashtra, the MSEB's revenues were nearly double that of 1992, not because of a doubling in the amount of electricity sold, (the increment is about 30 per cent), but due to the near doubling of power tariffs. Even after this doubling of tariffs, the MSEB still has to set aside 70 per cent of its revenues to be able to pay Enron.

Additionally, the MoU stipulated that Enron would be paid roughly the same amount of money whether the MSEB took 50 per cent, 75 per cent or 90 per cent of the plants capacity. The plant's capacity of 2015 MW amounted to 15 billion units a year. Maharashtra was selling 43 billion units a year then. Six years later, in 1996–97, the MSEB sold about 60 billion units.

The Government's Initial Approach

In June 1992, the GoM wrote to Enron reminding them of the provisions of the law. In particular they asked them to submit a break-up of project costs and the return of equity that was assumed. Enron wrote back on 13 July 1992, telling the GoM, that

> ...we would advise you against auditing project costs and predetermining return on equity.

It is pertinent to note, once again, that the return on equity was capped by law. Moreover, project costs required the approval of the CEA. This "advice" had been followed to date by the GoI, the GoM, the CEA as well as the MSEB.

In early August 1992, the Secretary of Power, Government of India requested the CEA to draw up an alternative least cost plan and to evaluate the project's technical grounds.

On 7 August, 1992, commenting on the scope of the Act vis-à-vis tariff and the proposed power purchase agreement the Chairman, CEA, wrote to the GoI, stating that:

> CEA concurrence under Section 31 is statutory and cannot perhaps be dispensed with...the sale price of energy and quantum of energy to be produced...(are)...aspects...to be examined by the CEA.

He expressed the need for an increase in capacity of this magnitude in Maharashtra. On 18 August 1992, the CEA was handed an additional responsibility—it was asked to "consider the total foreign exchange outgo".[23]

---

[23]Minutes of the second meeting of the 'High Powered Board' dated 18 August 1992.

4

Enron's Approach to Indian Law

The "Problems" with Law

The existing law had been modified in September 1991, specifically to increase private sector participation. After having signed the MoU, the next step in Enron's opinion was to immediately sign an agreement between itself and the MSEB. This was the PPA or the power purchase agreement.

In the light of requests that the project be examined as per the provisions of law, there seems to have been an internal examination of the framework of laws affecting utilities in the country. Enron's lawyer, a partner in the English firm of Linkletter and Paines, Mr Adrian Montague carried out an analysis of Indian laws. This culminated in a note dated 4 September 1992, addressed to the Secretary of Power, GOI.[24] A copy each of the notes was also sent and made

---

[24]Note dated 4.9.92 from Linklaters and Paines addressed to Shri Vasudavan, Secretary, Power.

available to all government agencies including the CEA, the MSEB and the GoM itself.

The title of the note is very revealing. It was called "The Problems Concerning the Application of the Indian Electricity Acts" (emphasis in the original). The "object of this note" was "to highlight the problems that the provisions in these Acts raised for the Dabhol power project."

The first round of minor "problems" that were identified included the "power of the MSEB and the CEA to regulate DPC activities"; that the DPC would "have to follow all directions of MSEB". This would be a "problem as the PPA itself" provided for "a dispute resolution process", and that "the CEA" which was an "administrative agency, should have powers to exercise judicial functions in disputes between the DPC and the MSEB".

One of the key "problems" identified were the "tariff regulations" published by the government. These were found by Enron to be "incompatible with the financial structure of a power station project". They were found to be problematic particularly because of "the assumed load factors"; the "admissibility of foreign exchange variations"; "the permitted return on equity"; and "the five year term of the tariff". The DPC wanted an assurance that there would be "...no risk of regulatory interference in the rather different pricing provisions in the PPA."

Furthermore, "Section 18A of the 1948 Act" has "provisions for the duties of a generating company". These include duties of operating and maintaining the power station "in the most efficient and economical manner". Enron was concerned about the "the consequences of a breach of this duty". They wanted to know who "would enforce the duties?" At this stage, Enron had started thinking about "the remedies generally available under Indian Law for breach of statutory duty".

The last problem that was identified by Enron was that the

DPC, like any other limited company, would be required to abide by the provisions of the Companies Act. However the Electricity Acts contained "further reporting requirements" including the provision that the "generating company" should "furnish to the CEA...accounts, statistics, returns of other information relating to the generation, supply and use of electricity..."

The solicitors offered a range of "solutions". These included "amending legislation". This solution however, was considered to be "politically impracticable", and a more "acceptable solution" was found to be the "administrative direction" or "notifications". These notifications, it was held, would be able to "modify the tariff structure published under Section 43-A". Alternatively, the GoI and/or MSEB could sign "contractual undertakings" "regarding the practical application of the relevant provisions in the case of the Dabhol Power Project". In the last resort, the GoI and/or the MSEB's advisers could "issue...legal opinions."

The Official Response

The MSEB responded to this note two weeks later on 21 September 1992. Basing its letter "on advice of our legal experts", it said

> ...DPC...*will have cast upon it statutory duties and to that extent is likely to be subject in the due performance of such duties to public and judicial scrutiny. This may not be acceptable to foreign promoters... One such area of scrutiny would be...under Section 18-A 'to operate and maintain' in the most efficient and economical manner, the generating stations...* (Emphasis in the original).

The chairman then forwarded the note to the GoI and in turn set out Enron's conditions. After "joint discussions between Enron, the MSEB and the Government of

Maharashtra", between 23 and 26 September, the chairman of the MSEB wrote to the Joint Secretary (IPC), Government of India on 30 September. He reiterated that

> *public and judicial scrutiny of business policy and decisions as per the Act will not be acceptable by a company like DPC* (emphasis supplied).

Attitude to Law

Ordinarily, after having signed the MoU, the matter should have ended. But one of the most surprising aspects of this affair is Enron's attitude towards the law. Even more surprising is the government's reaction to Enron's explicitly stated position. From the very beginning Enron's attitude was one of arrogance and an open disdain for the law.

This letter is probably the most decisive point in the Enron saga. The letter is instructive in that its matter-of-fact tone is the prelude to the future attitude of the company. The assumption underlying this letter was the severe limitations of the laws of India. The title itself, the 'problems with Indian laws' is a statement in arrogance.

It does not seem to have struck anyone that all persons are subject to laws in India and are bound to comply with them. Also, that all persons, no matter who they are, are subject to judicial review and scrutiny.

In any other country, under similar circumstances, the company would have been asked to leave. In its home country, with its considerably stringent laws and reporting requirements, writing such a letter would perhaps have put a few Enron executives behind bars. Business houses function within existing national laws. They may circumvent them, or use existing loopholes within them to their own advantages. They may go as far as flaunting them. But the complete dismissal of national laws is noteworthy.

One of the key failures, deliberate or otherwise of the Indian system, has been to treat this company as if they were doing us a big favour. It is as if the country would not be able to survive without them. Any criticism, valid or otherwise was and is still treated as an affront not only to the tenets (whatever those may be) of liberalisation but as anti-business or anti-multinational.

Foreign investment is a classic red herring. They are supplying us with a commodity at their price. Of course they are making an investment. Even the suppliers of say, erasers or guns or whatever, to the government, have to put up some money to set up a factory, get raw materials, machinery and the rest of it. At no stage does one talk of it as an investment that the supplier is putting up. It was and is simply a supplier selling his wares.

In contrast, consider the behaviour of any country in the world when it comes to making purchases. China by dangling carrots of purchases amounting to a few billion dollars, manages to get the heads of nearly every major corporation in the USA to pressurize the Congress and the Presidency to get the trade terms that it seeks. Even the sheikdoms of the Persian gulf, possess far greater panache and of course—self respect. The country that is trying to sell, practically begs and pleads. The president of the USA deputes his vice-president to convince the Saudis to buy their arms over, say the French, for relatively small purchases of arms amounting to a few billion dollars.

Enron had signed an MoU with the MSEB for the supply of electricity at the price that they had asked for, they were to supply us with a commodity, in this case electricity, and we were and will have to pay them for it. This single purchase of electricity by the state of Maharashtra however, amounts to well over US $30 billion at the very least.

Last, but not the least Enron's demand that they should not be subjected to scrutiny of any kind, notwithstanding the law, is noteworthy. Even for a moment, if one sets aside the question of Law, elementary common sense dictates that a purchase of a commodity by anyone, the state or a private party can be subject to scrutiny—is the price appropriate, how much does one need, in what quantities, at what time and, of course, can one afford to pay for it? Finally, is the purchase in conformity with the provisions of the law?

5

Managing the World Bank

The World Bank's Opinion

To secure finances for the project, the finance ministry approached the World Bank. On March 12, 1993, the ministry formally requested the World Bank to consider financing the project.

In the light of the request from the GoI, the WB examined the proposed Dabhol Power Project of the Enron Power Development Corporation. The report of the World Bank, dated 30 April, 1993, was sent to the finance ministry.[25]

The Secretary of Finance forwarded the note to the Secretary of Power, requesting him to take note that the "comments of the Bank", were "examined expeditiously". He went on to request the ministry of power that, if necessary, the "project be recast in the light of their observations".

The Detailed Analysis

The detailed analysis of the bank is set out below. In its note the World Bank initially assured the ministry of finance that

---

[25]Note dated 30.4.93 from the World Bank to the Secretary, Finance.

it strongly supported the "government's private power initiatives". However, it went on to indicate that the MSEB would "have no option but to run the plant in base-load" since the plant was "designed to consume the output of one LNG train". This addition of a 2015 MW station, in "forced base-load operation" would place "a significant constraint in MSEB's power system". It said that while the project would provide "additional generation" which would help increasing loads in peak periods, it would consequently "displace lower cost coal-fired generation in the off-peak periods".

Bringing the project as a base-load station would "worsen the already existing imbalance between base-load generation (mainly coal) and peak-to-intermediate load generation (mainly hydro supplemented by natural gas in combined cycle generation). There would be surplus power in the off-peak periods." At best, the MSEB would be able to sell coal-based power in the southern region, at or close to its variable generating cost, in off-peak periods. As a result it would incur financial losses.

LNG generation at a variable cost of about paise 150/kWh would displace coal-based power costing paise 30/kWh. This loss, adjusted to economic terms, would have to be included in the economic analysis as a project cost and thus reduce project benefits.

Natural gas-fired combined cycle stations provide an appealing option for intermediate to base load generation. In the Indian system, given the current and the projected availability of lower cost coal fired base load generation during off-peak periods, combined cycle stations are economically attractive mainly in intermediate load service. In the WB's opinion "targeting the Dabhol Project to take advantage of this niche would require modifications in the project design and size as well as in the PPA" would have been a better option.

On the issue of the "cost and value of LNG Power", the World Bank concluded that consumers would not be willing or able to pay such a price for LNG power from Enron, and therefore, the "Bank's standard project economic analysis" concluded "that the project is not viable".

The project's "only justification" would be as a "special effort to meet the electricity demands of consumers expressing a willingness to pay higher tariffs for guaranteed and/or additional supply at system peak periods". However, no estimate for such expensive power was actually done. Additionally, this would involve "substantial tariff adjustments" for the MSEB. "Prices for industrial consumers would at the minimum have to be doubled in nominal terms to recover the cost of LNG power" and an "across the board adjustment" of tariffs made to all categories of customers and not just industrial ones, with "annual increases" of about "15–20 per cent against the Bank's 5–6 per cent inflation estimates".

Enron had indicated to the World Bank that the total cost of power was "about US cents 7.0/kWh". This figure was completely inaccurate. However, accepting the number at its face value, the bank calculated that the "resulting retail revenue from LNG power would have... (to be) equivalent to Rs 4.6/kWh in 1998 prices". This price to the consumer furthermore, did not leave any "provision for administrative and other MSEB overheads" or scope for any "cross-subsidization of agricultural and residential consumers".

According to the World Bank, the "implementation of the project would place a significant long-term claim on India's foreign exchange resources" with the "estimated annual fuel cost" being "about US $500 million, subject to escalation". The capacity payments in foreign currency would start at about US $175 million with a 70 per cent foreign exchange portion.

It assumed that the alternative to the LNG project would

be to build additional coal-fired stations using local coal. In this case the outflow in foreign exchange "would be significantly below those of the Enron project (about 30–40 per cent only of the Enron outflow)" and could be "even lower depending on the extent of domestic manufacturers' participation in the equipment supply". This was because the outflow would be "limited to debt service for foreign borrowing, foreign exchange".

The foreign exchange outflow resulting from the development of coal-fired generation using imported coal would be much closer to the outflows of the Enron project (the difference would depend on the source of equipment and the possibly different escalation of LNG and coal prices).

One of the arguments put up by the project's proponents was that in the absence of the project, India could not implement the domestic or the imported coal option, due to financing constraints. The World Bank's answer to that was that in any case "true additionality of the project is limited to the foreign equity", and that the "major part of the project financing proposed to be provided by the Bank, US Exim Bank and domestic capital market" should be "available to finance reasonable alternative projects, such as a series of 500 MW coal projects using imported coal".

The need for the project had been retrospectively created by the MSEB. It used a much higher rate of growth of power than the CEA which had conducted a detailed nationwide survey. This survey known as the 14th EPS (Electrical Power Survey) was used to plan future capacity expansions. In this the CEA had assumed an annual load growth of over 7 per cent in the 1990s and about 6 per cent in the following decade. The MSEB maintained that the CEA's projections were too low, on the basis of pending applications from industries for additional supply not considered in the CEA projection. Such applications rather conveniently amounted to exactly 4100 MW. The MSEB's assessment was that about

50 per cent of these applications would materialize, thus increasing the peak load by 2100 MW by 1997. This would absorb all the LNG power and eliminate the projected surpluses.

The bank considered these arguments and simply responded that "should this load scenario materialize, surpluses would indeed diminish. However, this would not invalidate the conclusion that an LNG-based power plant operating in base-load was not the least cost option for expanding power supply." It went on to demolish the MSEB's arguments completely. It concluded that the "suggested load increase is unproven and the proposed high forecast is not a suitable basis for evaluating the project."

The bank drew particular attention to three points regarding the proposed high forecast. First, the full additionality of the loads "in pending applications" was "questionable" and the "resulting growth rate for industrial electricity consumption unproven". Under the MSEB's proposed additional load to be connected by 1997, the key assumption was that industrial load would double, i.e., grow at an average rate of about 20 per cent for four years, compared to the CEA's already respectable 8 per cent average annual growth. Therefore the MSEB's argument was not sustainable. Second, the willingness of the applicants on the MSEB's 4100 MW list to pay a very high price, involving more than doubling of the then current industrial tariffs, was not tested. Before a high forecast could be adopted as the basis of the analysis of the new state-wide forecast, a review of the MSEB's own forecasts would need to be undertaken, taking price explicitly into account in the forecast. Third, the MSEB would be unable to connect the new load gradually between 1993 and 1997 as it did not have additional generation capacity. The load was unlikely to wait until 1996–1998 and then come in over a one or two year period. More likely the increase would be gradual.

It went on to explicitly state that "not proceeding with the project may somewhat delay power development, but it is unlikely to cause a lasting setback to India's private power programme."

The World Bank's Conclusions

"On the basis of the analysis detailed above, the World Bank reached the following conclusions:"

(a) The project is not a least-cost choice for base-load power generation compared to Indian coal and local gas. Even if domestic fuels are not available, imported coal would be the least-cost option for base-load generation for MSEB with current environmental standards. The additional requirement of fuel-gas desulphurisation would narrow coal's advantage, but in all likelihood not eliminate it; an environmental premium would be required to close the gap. In addition to lower fuel cost, the coal alternative is more attractive due to its flexibility, capacity can be added in 500 MW units in steps to meet the growing demand instead of the 2000 MW in 1998 in the project.

(b) The unique features and risks of this LNG-based project (large minimum consumption, dependence on one power generator and on one LNG supplier) need to be considered; they offset LNG's environmental benefits over coal. The LNG price escalation cost is still to be confirmed for the project; international practice is to link the price of LNG to oil or coal price.

(c) Enron's current proposal would require MSEB to dispatch the plant as a base-load unit at 80–85 per cent minimum plant factor (referred to as plant load factor, PLF, in India). This would prevent the operational flexibility of a combined cycle plant.

(d) Stipulations of MSEB power operations indicate that the

project would add more capacity than needed to meet the projected load growth in 1998 and would also result in uneconomic plant dispatch (lower variable cost coal power would be replaced by much higher variable cost LNG power). This would adversely affect the economic viability of the project and place a heavy financial burden on the MSEB; and,

(e) Substantial adjustment in electricity tariffs would be required to recover the cost of the project from the consumers and to safeguard MSEB's financial position. Given the large share of the project in MSEB's power supply in the initial years, across-the-board adjustments would be required. Adjustments limited to special industrial consumer categories would not be sufficient as their capability to continue to cross-subsidise, by paying more than the already high cost of LNG power, would be limited.

The State Government's Response

The state government's (as well as MSEB's) response to the World Bank's analysis and conclusions is a revelation. True, the government and the MSEB were trying to defend the indefensible, however, the level of incompetency that emerges is quite remarkable.

A month after having received the World Bank's analysis, the Secretary of the Industries, Energy & Labour Department, on "behalf of the Government of Maharashtra", added "the following points" in their letter to the government of India. They start off by saying that the World Bank's

> note does not support the Project. It, however, points out very clearly that this project would be a very good project if it was not coming up in India. (Emphasis supplied)

After having made this observation, the GoM interpreted

the WB analysis to say that the World Bank was "not satisfied mainly on the ground that the demand does not justify setting up of a large project and that the project would create financial difficulties for MSEB". Though the bank's "conclusion appear to be prima facie reasonable", the World Bank had not taken into cognisance factors like the "MSEB would have to improve its grid discipline to absorb the Enron power", and that the MSEB had "to improve its general working as well".

The "assessment of the World Bank seems to say that the Enron Project would put a heavy financial burden on MSEB and that the project is not a part of the least cost sequence for power generation in Maharashtra". However, the secretary interpreted this conclusion to mean that "it is interesting that the World Bank feels that imported coal and not LNG would be a better option for base-load station of MSEB. The enclosed note of Mr Vergin's letter brings out very clearly that the cost of Enron Project compares favourably with the cost of imported coal fired generation unit".

He goes on to say that "The World Bank presumes that the tariff of the LNG based power project from Enron will be very high. It is necessary to carry out the analysis separately," [It is] "our belief is that the tariff that MSEB would charge to its consumers would compare favourably with the projected tariff. We are, however, negotiating strongly with Enron Power Corporation and trying to push down the tariff." Not only did the GoM have no clue as to what the tariff was, but after negotiating strongly, the tariff in fact increased.

The bank had made a factual observation. At night there was (and is to date) surplus capacity in the western region. In response, the secretary stated that "it is not right to say that there is a large surplus capacity during the off peak hours. In any case, even the pit mouth coal plants in the State have stocks only for a day or two. Conserving their stocks during the off peak hours will actually enable MSEB to meet the peak demand little more efficiently." And he further went on to say that "we are confident that the Enron project can easily run as a base-load station."

The GoM was seriously advocating "conserving" coal based power whose variable cost was 30–40 paisa a unit, to justify LNG power whose minimum variable cost would be Rs 1.50. Of course the Enron station can be run as a base- load station but doing so would not only endanger the entire system and cause enormous financial losses but would also accentuate the already existing problems of the shortage of peaking power. An analysis by the CEA had indicated that the amount of backing down would amount to as much as 408 MW even in the initial phase of 695 MW. A coal based station because of its inherent limitation,[26] cannot be run as a peaking station. The World Bank's note states quite clearly that it would be more prudent to modify the proposed PPA and use the intrinsic capabilities of a gas based station to run it as a peaking to intermediate load station if at all they were to go ahead with the project.

The note ends with a request that the "Government of India should take up the matter strongly with the World Bank and ask them to review their decision" as their "comments may create a problem for the developers to raise commercial and institutional borrowings."

The other bank arguments particularly about the economics of the project are not alluded to.

A reading of the above either indicates that the GoM had not understood even marginally, the World Bank analysis, or,

---

[26]Peaking power is the short sudden surge in demand that a power system has to be geared to face. A gas station takes very little time to build at full capacity as opposed to a coal based station which literally takes two weeks to be fired up. Once fired up, it takes about the same amount of time to be shut down. The difference can be seen to be akin to a gas based stove and the coal based chulas.

alternatively, a decision to push through the project by its proponents at any cost whatsoever. A combination of both these possibilities seems to be the explanation.

The MSEB's Response

The MSEB's justification is on roughly similar lines. In an internal note around the same time, the MSEB forecast a steep decline in its operational efficiency and system in order to justify the Enron project.

> *In our comments...we had also brought out the problems of coal shortages, low quality of coal and inadequate supply of gas leading to reduction in the availability of the existing capacity.*
>
> *Although the World Bank analysis had stated that "MSEB will have no option but to run the plant in base load with minimum variation", this was not true since in their "discussions with ENRON, they have agreed to despatch the output to suit the system requirement."*

This was and is a lie. The contract and all discussions from day one stated quite clearly that the plant would be a base load plant.

The MSEB's note went on to say that "in the case of coal based stations" "reducing their loads during off-peak hours would help in conserving maximum loads during the day peaks".

"The construction period for a coal based plant will be around 60 to 72 months as compared to 30 months of an LNG based combined cycle plant. This will increase the capital due to larger interest during construction".

The level of incompetence inherent in the analysis amounts to a dereliction of duty and malfeasance.

Changing World Bank Opinion and Managing the Media

In early June 1993, the World Bank note was leaked to the

press. Snippets from the bank's analysis were carried in most newspapers. The resulting controversy nearly derailed the project.

In response to the World Bank's analysis and increasing press criticism, Joseph Sutton, the Vice President of Enron wrote to the Chairman, MSEB, that

> "*I feel that the World Bank opinion can be changed. We will engage a PR firm during the next trip and hopefully manage the (Indian) media from here on*".[27] (Emphasis Supplied)

The World Bank Remains Unmoved

The GoM and the MSEB had sent their reactions together with an analysis trying to refute the WB's conclusions and justify the project's existence to the WB.

On 26 July 1993, the World Bank replied to the GoI and MSEB. The bank did not change its "opinion". It went on to reiterate its earlier stand and severely criticised the MSEB's attempts to justify the project on grounds that its own system would decline in efficiency.

> However, we cannot accept the more pessimistic scenario recently provided by MSEB according to which the existing system is projected to decline in efficiency. If this were to be indeed the current best projection, determined actions should be taken with priority to reverse this projected deterioration rather than accepting it as a given fact in the analysis of new investments.
>
> …We are finding it difficult to accord supplied justification to the Dhabol [*sic*] project based on the most recently discovered slippages in MSEB's ongoing and planned least cost progress.
>
> After extensive further review of the above parameters and

---

[27]Letter dated 28 June 1993, from Joseph Sutton, Vice President of Enron to the Chairman, MSEB.

detailed review of the analytical framework and costing assumptions, we reconfirm our earlier conclusion that the Dabhol project as presently formulated is not economically justified and thus could not be financed by the Bank.

The Death Knell?

Many conventional critiques seem to put the blame for almost all problems that befall this country on the combine of the World Bank, the IMF and the GATT. Without going into any of the overtly simplistic arguments, a strong case atleast in this particular instance, can be made in favour of the World Bank.

The World Bank's analysis of the Dabhol power project is a strong critique. It was and is to date, the most coherent critique of the project and its consequences. The entire analysis was done in purely economic terms.

It has been the World Bank's institutional and operating mandate to support, expand and if necessary, force the entry of foreign private capital into countries that were averse to such an entry. This was particularly true in the eighties. The dramatic change in India's path was imposed by the World Bank's conditionalities to the loan agreements.

It is in this context, that the analysis of the World Bank is particularly important as well as being unequivocal. One would have presumed that the World Bank's detailed, rational and even, irrefutable critique should have sounded the death knell of the project.

6

The Project is Cleared

The Question of CEA Clearance

To facilitate the signing of the formal agreement, the law had mandated that the price of power and the technical aspects of the project be cleared by the CEA. The company had made it quite clear that it did not want to have the price it had set down examined by anyone. In particular, it wanted to do away with CEA clearance, since that would have meant disclosing facts that it would rather not. It was trying to sign the agreement with the MSEB without the necessary 'techno-economic' clearance of the CEA.

The CEA was also asked by the MSEB whether it could go ahead and simply sign an agreement with Enron for the purchase of power. The CEA was being forced to issue an official clarification. The CEA wrote[28] to the GoI stating that its "concurrence under Section 31" was "statutory" and could not "be dispensed with".

The MSEB had insisted that it should be allowed to sign the contract with Enron and thereafter seek clearance. In

---

[28]Letter dated 7 August 1992, from the CEA to the GoI.

response, the CEA pointed out that there were "difficulties in making the PPA subject to CEA clearance". Normally, the agreement to purchase power would have to "specify the sale price of energy" as well as the "quantum of energy to be produced". Both these aspects had to be "examined by the CEA". It was possible that the CEA, after examining the project report, would suggest "modifications in respect of sale price" or in the "quantum of energy" to be produced. This could lead to a "breach of agreement". Additionally, based on its own analysis and the data it had accumulated, the CEA was concerned about the need for such an increase of capacity in Maharashtra.

In March 1993, the quest for some sort of a clearance from the CEA resumed in earnest. Interestingly enough, at around the same time the company had, just informed the government that since it was in no position to procure gas supplies, it would break up the project into two phases. The first phase of 695 MW would use diesel as a fuel.[29] Thereafter,

---

[29]Enron had trouble procuring the gas the station was supposed to be running on. It failed in its attempts to secure a definite tie-up with any gas suppliers. It therefore decided to come up with another project altogether and declared its intentions of breaking up the project into two phases: an initial first phase of 695 MW to be run on distillate #2 (diesel) followed by another phase of 1440 MW. With the commencement of the second phase, both phases would run on LNG.

When Enron first came to India, all permissions given to it were obtained on the basis of a plant using liquefied natural gas as a fuel. Instead Enron now proposed to run the first phase on a banned fuel—diesel. Diesel was banned for use in any large scale generation of power. This plan to run the plant on diesel was formally proposed by Enron and the government did not object. It simply agreed.

On 16 March 1993, Enron simply informed the government that the project had changed completely and that the project was now changed to an initial 695 MW plant which would use diesel as the fuel. The project would be run on LNG after arrangements were made for the supply of gas. (*contd.*)

Enron submitted a document purporting to be a project report[30] to the CEA in April 1993. The project report did not reveal any of the critical parameters required for the evaluation of the project. Some of these missing parameters include the costing of components of the project, the rate of interest, etc.

The CEA was in a quandary. It was faced with extraneous pressures and/or inducements to clear the project. The CEA was supposed to examine the tariff, the cost of the project and the consequences of the project on the system in Maharashtra while according or refusing to accord "techno-economic clearance".

Consider one aspect of the CEA's quandary. The cost of the project,[31] at least as notified publicly, was Rs 9,053 crore.

(*contd.*) The then Secretary of Power, GoI, wrote to the GoM that Enron had obtained all permissions on the basis of an LNG plant. He pointed out that the absence of gas supply tie-ups had always been an issue. He reminded them of the earlier communications from the Ministry of Power emphasising the need to ensure that Enron had proper LNG tie-up. He went on to point out that this should not have come as a surprise since the World Bank, the MoP and others had already indicated that LNG would not be available.

The breakup of the project in two phases came to be quite handy in future court cases. The government and the MSEB then swore on oath that the project was broken up to take heed of the World Bank's criticism.

[30]The report gave some technical details

Main gas turbines: STAG 209 FA (otherwise referred to as 9FA) frames, steam turbines, black start (cold start) and peaking power from 6B frames and a heat recovery steam generator. The nominal rating of the phase I frame was 748 MW. The fuel facility was to be owned and managed by a separate entity. Fuel cost was specified as US $ 3.8 linked to shipping and oil indices. The heat rate guaranteed by DPC was 7605 BTU/kWh (for distillate) whereas the heat rate guaranteed by the contractor is 7243 BTU/kWh. The heat rate guaranteed is the heat rate of 9F frames, not 9FA. Further, any change in heat rate will be deemed to be "change in costs" and therefore as an increase in tariff.

[31]In the public notification, the total cost of the project was stated to be Rs 9053 crores. The widely differing and always increasing cost of (*contd*)

This works out to Rs 4.49 crore per MW. In August 1993 the CEA had conducted a detailed evaluation[32] of the reasonable capital cost of CCGT[33] plants, (like Enron). The CEA study considered all relevant factors including currency depreciation, interest during construction, the average rate of inflation etc. The study showed the reasonable capital cost of a CCGT plant to be Rs 1.81 crore per MW (December 1996 completed costs) and Rs 1.91 crore per MW (December 1997 completed costs).[34] This is against Enron's cost (both then and currently) of over Rs 4.49 crore/MW.

The difference is astonishing, even after factoring in "other costs". It is particularly pertinent to note that after five years, the Ministry of Power, in September 1997, officially conceded that the reasonable capital costs of a CCGT plant were in the range of 1.8 crore/MW and not Rs 4.5 to 5.5 crore/MW. However, all agreements and MoUs still continue at the old rates.

Bypass the CEA?

There was enormous pressure on the CEA from bureaucrats and politicians to clear the project inspite of patently obvious deficiencies of all kinds—legal, technical and economic. There was no way the project could be cleared in accordance with the law.

A decision was then taken by Sharad Pawar, the Chief Minister (CM) of Maharashtra, that the CEA would be bypassed completely and no heed given to the misgivings raised by it or for that matter the World Bank and others.

(*contd.*) the project given by Enron to different authorities at different points of time is interesting.

[32]CEA's evaluation of bids for DESU's Bawana project. Internal Evaluation dated August 1993.

[33]Combined Cycle Gas Turbine.

[34]"Rs. 18130 per kW (December 1996) and Rs. 19160 per kW (December 1997)".

In August 1993, in a meeting[35] the CM put forth a proposition that issues like the "import of fuel", total "foreign exchange outgo" and (presumably) tariff "were minor issues to be clarified", and that "the Foreign Investment Promotion Board (FIPB) would take a decision on them at the time of final review".

The intial official reaction of the Ministry of Power was to reject this suggestion. The Union Minister for Power seems to have rejected Pawar's suggestion and explicitly stated that the "project need(ed) to be techno-economically appraised and cleared by the CEA before the MSEB signs any formal agreement with the Company". He also stated that "the project should be in conformity [with] the point of view of the existing guidelines with particular reference to two-tier tariff". However, this seemed to have changed later.

Moving Forward on the Issue

On 26 August 1993, Rebecca Mark of Enron, expressing satisfaction over the progress of the project wrote to Sharad Pawar, stating

> The remaining concern seems to reside with Mr Beg, Member, Planning for Thermal Projects (the CEA). He continues to hold up project approval based on the question of demand for power in Maharashtra. No one from the Ministry of Power in Delhi has given direction to Mr Beg to move forward on this issue.

It is clear that Enron was asking Pawar to intercede and influence a statutory body in the discharge of its duties and/or to get the Ministry of Power to do so against the informed judgment of the expert authority.

---

[35]Meeting of the high powered board in August 1993.

The CEA Receives a Letter

On 11 November, 1993, the day before the CEA was to meet to consider granting or refusing clearance to the project, it received a letter from the Ministry of Power,[36] simply stating that

> Finance Secretary observed that the question of cost of power had been looked into and it had been found that it was more or less in line with other projects being put up in Maharashtra.

The letter seemed to state that the Finance Secretary had examined the cost of the project and found it to be reasonable. Neither is the Finance Secretary competent to examine this aspect, nor is he empowered by law or statute to examine it. In any case, there were also no similar projects in Maharashtra, in India, or for that matter anywhere in the world.

The CEA was effectively being told not to examine the costs of the project.

The History of the Letter

A decision had been taken at the highest levels to simply subvert the existing provisions of the law. The FIPB, a body that had neither the competence nor the legal authorisation, would simply consider the various "issues" and dispose off them.

These issues include "the primary concern" tariff of and other issues like "the guaranteed purchase and assumptions about 90% PLF" that would imply that "other stations with cheaper power may have to back down while Dabhol would not".

On 2 November, the FIPB had noted that one of the key issues was the "reasonableness of the tariff formula" and that "there had been some criticism of the high cost of power"

---

[36]Letter from the Secretary Power, GoI addressed to the Chairman, CEA.

from this project. The cost of the project was clearly very high, over twice the cost of any other project in the world. This mattered because the final cost of power depended on the cost of the project. The difference in costs amounted to a few thousand crore. The organisations (the World Bank and in particular the CEA) that had examined the project proposal had noted that the price of power was very high and in breach of all existing laws and norms. Further, the addition of a base-load capacity of this magnitude would result in the backing down of much cheaper coal power.

It was noted in the meeting that the "the Central Electricity Authority would go into the question of reasonability of tariff and the principles of tariff formula". However, it was decided that the CEA would not prove to be a deterrence but simply be bypassed.

The FIPB Holds a Meeting

The "key issue" and the "primary concern" about the cost of power was hastily and perfunctorily disposed of in the following manner.

The next day, 3 November, 1993, the Finance Secretary, GoI, convened a meeting on the Dabhol Power Project to discuss "the tariff for power proposed by M/s Enron". The recorded minutes of the meeting tell a rather interesting story. The people present in that meeting were from all concerned and unconcerned ministries.[37]

The Finance Secretary sought a "clarification" on the "exact nature of the tariff" proposed by the company. In response

---

[37]From the Ministry of Finance, the Finance Secretary and the Chief Economic Adviser to the Ministry. The Ministry of Power was represented by the Secretary, Power, the Special Secretary, and Director. The GoM was represented by the Chairman, MSEB, the Finance Adviser MSEB and the Chief Engineer of MSEB. The PMO was represented by the Dt. Secy. and the Director. The Revenue Secretary was also present.

the Financial Adviser, MSEB[38] stated that it was not a "one part dollar tariff" but had been broken down into various cost components. The estimated starting tariff was 7.5 cents per unit in 1997, with "an approximate 95 per cent dollar linkage". The tariff escalated over time at about 4 per cent p.a. in dollar terms, i.e., about 12 to 14 per cent in rupee terms.

Thereafter the Finance Secretary sought a clarification on the "Internal Rate of Return (IRR) on equity assumed in the calculations" for the tariff. In response the Financial Adviser MSEB, stated that the "normal IRR to investors would be 25.22 per cent" and "assuming an inflation rate of around 3 to 4 per cent, the real IRR would be 20.6 per cent at 80 per cent availability."

This means that the return on equity was of the order of 32 per cent pre-tax. The law allowed a return of 16 per cent. The IRR works out (very approximately) to over a 32 per cent return on equity. The law, mandated a 16 per cent return on equity. Every 1 per cent return on equity represents a return of US $8.5 million (Rs 28 crore) in a project this size. The overall difference amounts to about US $140 million every year for a twenty-year contract on this single count alone.

---

[38]Shri Mathrani's entry as the financial adviser, MSEB is one of those stories. In an internal 'secret' note, a panel of secretaries of the GoM had noted that there were 'problems' associated with him due to a possible linkage in the securities scam (He was associated with Standard Chartered Bank). In September 1992 the MSEB had shortlisted a prestigious panel of international bankers to act as advisers in the negotiations with Enron. Mr. Mathrani's company suddenly appears, retrospectively, in the shortlist. The five international firms with the necessary technical and financial expertise disappear from the reckoning and Mr. Mathrani is abruptly "selected" as the "Financial Advisor to the MSEB" inspite of having no previous experience in the power sector, nor the technical competence. Since then, Mr. Mathrani has been a "leading" consultant. Numerous reports on the power sector have been commissioned from his firm by the finance ministry.

The Chairman, MSEB, interjected to state that "in the negotiations they had attempted to bring down this rate but had eventually accepted this figure."

The question was raised as to whether "this was an unreasonable rate of return". It was, therefore considered necessary to examine the "validity of the cost estimates". The Financial Adviser, MSEB, stated that "they were not competent to comment on capital costs". He, however, went on to suggest that he "felt" that these "were not out of line". The Chairman, MSEB, explained that the "costs of the Enron project" were "not viewed as substantially higher than those received through competitive bidding".

This general, unsubstantiated statement was simply accepted at face value.

The minutes, thereafter, go on to record "that the costs were more or less on par with that of other projects".

This sentence is particularly important. The meeting was held over a year after the MoU was signed. There no examination of the cost of the project, and deliberately false, arbitrary and misleading claims were being put forward. A rather general and dishonest statement after having conceded that they were "not competent" to "comment on them" in the first place was deliberately accepted and a false conclusion that the costs were more or less on par with other projects was recorded. To reiterate, these were no similar projects in Maharashtra or for that matter anywhere in the world.

Thereafter the discussion veered to the question of the "reasonableness" of such an exorbitant rate of profit. The law had allowed a 16 per cent return on equity. The additional profits over and above those allowed by the law, work out to about US $3 billion (Rs 10,000 crore rupees) over the life of the contract.

The Financial Adviser to the MSEB stated that "a reduced

IRR could facilitate a negotiation on reduced escalation for capacity charge on the tariff amounting to 0.57 cents/kWh."

Interestingly enough, a reduction of "0.57 cents/kWh," in a situation of "a reduced IRR" amounts to US $90 million a year (Rs 300 crore a year). No such "reduction", however took place.

The Finance Secretary asked about the "tariff in the Hub River project of Pakistan". The Financial Adviser, MSEB stated that in the Hub River Project, there was a front loading of tariff which declined gradually over the years, and that the annualised tariff would be 5.9 cents per unit. By way of comparison "after excluding import duties and corporate taxes and removing the inflation element," the annualised tariff for Enron would be around 5.71 cents per unit while that for Hub Valley would be 5.4 cents per unit at 75 per cent PLF including 10 per cent import duties. This was because of the lower IRR of the Hub River Project. However, the annualised front loaded tariff of Hub Valley in Pakistan would be 5.9 cents/unit. This was against the annualised tariff of Dabhol which was 7.5 cents/unit and not 5.71 cents as dishonestly represented.

In addition, the 7.5 cents tariff of the DPC was back loaded. Consequently, the Hub Valley tariff went down over the years while Enron's tariff increased. No one sought to enquire why the IRR (which is lower than the average rate of return) for the Dabhol Project was so high in the first place, particularly in comparison to Pakistan.

Inspite of knowing very well that the tariff was not fixed and absolutely no risk was being taken by the company, the 'august gathering' came to this fallacious and debatable conclusion. The meeting simply ended by taking "note of the positive feature of the project" which included the "high plant load factor" and "a fixed tariff with risk being borne by the company". The meeting did not refer to the backing down of much cheaper coal stations, and instead insidiously misrepresented the high PLF of the Dabhol plant as a positive feature. Other equally critical issues like the very high cost of fuel, the import of fuel, the impact of the rupee depreciating etc. were simply not raised.

The Cost of Power Looked into

Two days later, in the next meeting of the FIPB,[39] based on the earlier discussion, it was simply recorded that:

> Finance Secretary observed that the question of cost of power had been looked into and it had been found that it was more or less in line with other projects being put up in Maharashtra...

In the same meeting, the Secretary (Power) "indicated" that CEA clearance "should be available in the week beginning 8th November, 1993". The CEA without having a chance to consider any aspect of the project had been forced, or induced to grant clearance to the project.

The CEA's Own Analysis of the Project

Despite the incompleteness of information in the project report submitted by Enron, the CEA carried out its own analysis.[40] The analysis came to the conclusion, inter alia, that the "minimum charges payable by MSEB" worked out to "1334.18 million dollars in the year 1998". At the rates of exchange prevailing then, this worked out to Rs 4268 crore in the first year.

The analysis went on to point out that the permission given to Enron for the repatriation of foreign exchange was limited to a total annual outflow of foreign exchange on all counts of US$ 950 million. The difference between the amount for which permission was given and the actual minimum outflow

---

[39]On 5.11.93 (recorded in the minutes dated/drawn on 10.11.1993).
[40]Analysis of the CEA, dated 8.11.93.

in the first year itself is startling. It amounts to nearly US $400 million a year or 40 per cent over the permitted amount. Therefore the CEA went on to suggest that the MSEB needed to deal with this startling discrepancy.

Enron had given highly inflated capital costs for the project. On these inflated costs, as per the CEA, the return on equity worked out to "26 per cent in the 5th year increasing to 52 per cent during the 15th year". The law has set the return on equity at 16 per cent. Every 1 per cent of return in equity translates to about 30 crore rupees a year. Due to the admittedly inflated capital costs, the actual equity brought into the project is less than claimed. Therefore the effective return on equity is substantially higher. It works out to be a few hundred per cent guaranteed in dollars for the next twenty years.

A comparison of the DPC tariff with the tariff as calculated under the law was also made by simply taking prices as "indicated by DPC". Even after allowing an ad-hoc incentive for the GoI tariff, the GoI tariff was lower by 14 paisa. The annual difference between the tariff as allowed by the law and Enron's privately negotiated tariff is of the order of Rs 220 crore (US $70 million) a year. Without the ad-hoc incentive the difference works out to an annual difference of the order of Rs 500 crore, i.e., over the life of the contract, in dollar terms, to nearly US $3000 million (Rs 100,000 crore).

The CEA also carried out a study of the backing down of existing generating stations. As per the CEA's analysis, a substantial amount of MSEB's own generating capacity would have to be backed down in order to accommodate the 90 per cent guarantee promised to Enron. As per the CEA, 408 MW of MSEB's generating capacity, in the first year, costing 50 paisa to 80 paisa a unit would be backed down to buy 695 MW of Enron's power at Rs 3.47 a unit (per MSEB).

Enron Responds to the CEA

The CEA was seriously concerned about the lack of any information, in particular the project costs and their breakdown. Enron had simply given a lump sum without giving an itemised breakup of individual components. The CEA repeatedly asked Enron to supply an itemisation of these costs.

Enron simply refused to supply the CEA with any information. In response to CEA's questions on the project costs, the DPC replied that

It is important to note...that capital costs are irrelevant to CEA".[41]

In response to the CEA asking for specific components involving an expenditure of nearly US $2.6 billion, (Rs 9000 crore then), the DPC's response was that

Your request for more detailed project costs of equipment/ system/works other than those provided in the capital cost summary cannot be supported and is not deemed necessary. (Emphasis supplied)

In reply to the CEA's request that "the reasons for the high cost of balance of plant and housing" be "furnished", DPC's response was same

as question #2 above. i.e. Your request...cannot be supported and is not deemed necessary.

The arrogance and total contempt for the law and legalities is noteworthy. At the least it would have seriously jeopardised any prospects for business in any country of the world, save India.

---

[41] 10.11.93, DPC's reply to the CEA.

Additional Issues before the CEA

According to its internal notes, the additional issues that the CEA had to consider before issuing a clearance to the project included the following:

— Non-typing up of essential clearances/inputs by Enron
— The non-justification of Phase II from the power absorption angle
— The costliest option of power generation
— The consequences of exemption of major deviation from Government of India Notification dated 30.3.1992

The CEA Issues a "Clearance"

On 12 November 1993, the CEA met to consider the project's techno-economic clearance. Here are some extracts from the minutes of that meeting:

Chairman stated that in view of the replies received from M/s DPC in regard to cost estimates, clarification by the Ministry of Power on financial package and the examination of tariff aspects by Ministry of Finance, examination by CEA would, in effect, get limited to the technical aspects and need for the project which was already discussed. Chief Engineer (C) expressed the view that given this background, the completed cost would not be considered by CEA at a later stage.

After discussion, it was decided that the Ministry of Power might be informed that in view of the fact that the tariff for power from the project was a negotiated one and not in conformity with GoI notification, and not related to the capital cost and cost of power from the project and that these had been looked into by the Ministry of Finance, (only the technical aspects of the scheme were examined in CEA and found to be generally in order). Formal communication of clearance to technical aspects of the scheme could be given after compliance of Section 29 of the Electricity

(Supply) Act, 1948 by M/s DPC subject to conditions set out therein. [Emphasis supplied]

Thus, from the documentary record, it is evident that the CEA consideration of the cost aspects of the Dabhol project resulted in an adverse conclusion drawn on all counts, viz. tariff, rate of return, forex outflow and heavy additional economic costs imposed upon the MSEB.

Faced with extraneous pressure to clear the project, the CEA abdicated its statutory responsibility to consider costs in their various aspects on the basis of the arbitrary, misleading and fraudulent letter from the MoP. Thus the CEA acted in breach of its statutory duty by examining only the technical aspects of the scheme, and deciding to accord, only technical clearance. Further, "that given this background, the completed cost would not be considered by CEA (even) at a later stage."

DPC Assured of Clearance

Ten days later, in their letter of 23 November 1993, the Ministry of Power told the DPC that it would "expedite consideration of all clearances which fall within" the ministry's "competence". It went on to give a blanket undertaking to the DPC that the ministry would "ensure that your application for such clearances are approved".

On 26 November 1993, the CEA gave clearance subject to certain conditions. In their letter the CEA specified that

Aspects relating to import of fuel, foreign exchange outgo and deivation from Government of India's notification including return on equity was looked into by FIPB and found acceptable by them.

The Official Position on the Clearance

On 2 December 1993, the Secretary (Energy) GoM, issued a note enclosing CEA's letter of 26 November 1993 holding that "This letter conveys full and final techno-economic clearance", and that "the project has been fully scrutinised by the Government of India who have now issued their final clearance".

Two days before the PPA was to be signed, the MSEB's solicitors clarified[42] that it was not a clearance at all. However, they suggested that an appropriate administrative notification could be issued to legalise the illegal retroactively.[43]

---

[42]Letter from Little and Co. to the MSEB dated 6.11.93.

[43]The question that is required to be considered in the light of the above communications is whether the scheme prepared by DPC for establishment of combined cycle LNG based thermal power plant of 2015 MW at Dabhol has the required approvals of the CEA as contemplated under the Electricity Supply Act, 1948.

In its communication dated 26 November, 1993 the CEA has only cleared the technical aspects, subject to conditions which have been reproduced above...in paragraph 2 of the letter of CEA it is observed that—

"The aspects relating to import of fuel, foreign currency exchange outgo and deviation from Government of India's tariff notification including return on equity have been examined by FIPB and the project has been found acceptable by them."

It is not clear from the above whether CEA itself has examined the issues relating to tariff in the context of the Government of India notification dated 30 March, 1992 and found the deviation there from acceptable to it.

The approval of tariff by the CEA assumes importance in the context of the overall techno-economic clearance of the Project which CEA is required to grantAs far as the tariff for the sale of electricity by generating company is concerned, the provisions are to be found under Section 43A(2) of the Supply Act. The said sub-section provides that the tariff for the sale of electricity by a Generating Company to the Board shall be determined in accordance with the norms regarding operation and the Plant Load Factor as may be laid down by the Authority and in accordance with the rates of Appreciation and reasonable return and such other factors as may be determined, from time to time, by the Central Government, by notification in the Official Gazettee. (*contd.*)

It must be emphasised that while the letter issued by the CEA was not a clearance, it was deliberately and repeatedly misrepresented as the 'techno-economic clearance. All parties including the GoI, the MSEB, the DPC and the CEA have claimed that this was clearance, on various occasions including to the Union Cabinet, the Cabinet of Maharashtra, the Courts, the Parliament and the Press as late as 1995.[44]

(*contd.*) The Central Government, in exercise of the powers conferred on it by the aforesaid provision by its notification dated 30th March, 1992 determined the factors in accordance with which the tariff for sale for electricity by generating companies to the Board and to other persons shall be determinedIt would be clear that the tariff for the sale of electricity which is agreed upon between DPC and the Board has to strictly conform to the norms laid down in the Government of India notifications.

If the tariff does not conform to the criteria then in our opinion it would be necessary for the CEA or the Government of India to specifically approve the tariff. As aforesaid the CEA has not approved the tariff but only noted that the deviation from the tariff notification has been examined and found acceptable by FIPB. This cannot amount to a clearance by the CEA of the PPA tariff formula

These matters, in our view, are not incapable of resolution especially since the FIPB has, according to the CEA, found the economic aspects of the project acceptable. This however, needs to be pursued at the appropriate level in the Government of India.

The Board, may in the meanwhile sign the PPA once the Government of Maharashtra approves it pursuant to the Chairman's request in that regard to the Secretary (Energy), subject to pursuing the matter of a formal Government of India notification relating to the tariff.

[44]All the parties now claim that the clearance was granted on 14 July 1994. However the following evidence suggests otherwise

1. A note for the Cabinet of the Government of India, drafted by the ministry of power, and seen and approved by the Minister of Power, dated 14 May, 1994 states that "the project has been approved by the CEA" i.e. the clearance had been granted before 14 May.

2. The Union Minister of Power had specifically noted in 1993 that "any formal agreement ought to be signed only after the CEA clears the project." The PPA (being a formal agreement and binding in part) was signed on 8.12.1993. (*contd.*)

This issue is of some import since the project was able to go ahead on a non-existent full "techno-economic clearance". To illustrate, the PPA was signed the week after. In retrospect, during the course of a court proceeding (see Chapter 16) all parties claimed that the clearance was issued in July 1994.

(*contd.*) 3. DPC in its affidavit in WP 1702 of 1994 (Ramdas Nayak & Anr. v. Union of India) had solemnly affirmed on 25.7.1994 i.e. after 14.7.1994 "The CEA approved the project on 26 November 1993 for the purposes of Section 29 of the Act..."

4. In the same petition, WP 1702 of 1994, in the Supplementary affidavit on behalf of Union of India and Ministry of Power, dated 16/8/94, affirmed that "The project was appraised by the Central Electricity Authority (CEA) and an "in principal" clearance was accorded by CEA on 20.09.93. CEA in this approval stated that "The scheme is found to be technically acceptable and the estimated cost is seen to be generally in order". CEA further scrutinized the project and held detailed discussions with Enron and accorded clearance on 12.11.93".

5. In the further affidavit of August 1994, the Chairman, MSEB had annexed and relied upon a press note in a press conference addressed by Ms. Rebecca Mark and Shri Nimbalkar (of the MSEB) dated 8 December 1993 which claimed that "The Central Electricity Authority of the GoI has issued a final clearance to the project". (i.e. before 8 December 1993).

6. The GoM's suit against DPC and MSEB refers to the project being cleared by the letter of 26.11.1993.

7. The GoM had also issued a note [Secretary (Energy) dated 2.12.1993] claiming that the project had been cleared and that the letter of 26.11.1993 was the "full and final clearance".

8. Further, the CEA itself, in its written submissions to the Joint Parliamentary Committee headed by Shri Jaswant Singh, MP stated that the clearance was granted on 26.11.1993 "In Case of Dabhol Power Project, on request of the company, in principle clearance was issued by the CEA in September 1993. In November 1993 CEA accorded clearance to the Dabhol Power project subject to fulfillment of certain conditions. On fulfillment of these conditions the CEA communicated its clearance to the project in July 1994". "In the meantime the Dabhol power company had been negotiating the tariff with GoM/MSEB. The tariff was finalised in December 1994. There is no departure from statutory stipulations".

7

The Tariff Mystery

Meanwhile in Maharashtra

The GoM had thrown all its weight behind trying to push the project through at all costs. From July 1993 onwards, there was a series of correspondence between various departments of the GoM, particularly the Department of Industries and Energy and the Department of Finance. This was to finalise a note prepared by the Department of Industries and Energy for the Cabinet of Maharashtra, seeking the cabinet's approval to allow the MSEB to sign the PPA. The CEA was still scrutinising the project. The finalisation of the note took about three months and there were a series of draft notes prepared that were circulated to various departments, particularly the Department of Finance. The department had raised a number of points about the proposed agreement. This cabinet note had been discussed between the MSEB, the Department of Energy and the Department of Finance, Government of Maharashtra, since July 1993. The note revealed startling discrepancies in the tariff figures for the project. Extracts from three different tables prepared over different periods of time are quoted below.

Table 1

The main features of the project are as follows:		
Phase II		*Phase I*
1. Installed Capacity		
Base Load MW	625	1280
Peaking Load MW	70	40
Total MW	695	1320
2. Fuel	Distillate No 2	LNG with distillate
oil as back up		
3. Year of Operation	1996	1998
4. Capital cost including import duties and		
sales tax in million $		
a. Power plant	745	1385
b. Harbour	35	32
c. Fuel storage and Regassification	45	428
d. Financing fee and working capital	39	120
Total US million $	864	1965
Rs in core		
(1 US $ = Rs. 32)	2765	6288
5. Tariff-all in one price at zero duty	(1996 level)	(1998 level)
cents/kWh	7.15	6.72
Rs/kWh	2.29	2.15
6. *Tariff all in one price with 20%*		
customs duty on equipments, 15% on		
fuel and sales tax		
Cents/kWh	7.94	7.82
Rs/kWh	2.54	2.50

The next note contains the following table.

Table 2

"it will be seen from the above that the tariff at the end of Phase I at the project site will be Rs. 2.54 per unit and Rs. 2.50 at the end of Phase II. This tariff, however, is the all in one price and includes cost of a major Harbour, fuel...

— Base load capacity of 625 MW and peaking capacity 70 MW—Phase I

— Total base load capacity of 1905 MW and peaking capacity 110 MW—Phase II

— The availability for the base load is taken at 90% and peaking capacity at 50%

— *Import duty of 20% on capital equipment and 30% on LNG and 7% on distillate*

18. The tariff worked out is as under:

Item	Tariff	
	Phase I *1996 Level*	*Phase II* *1998 Level*
Capacity charge cents/kWh	3.99	4.39
Energy charge cents/kWh	3.95	3.43
Total charge cents/kWh	7.94	7.82
Rs/kWh at Rs. 32 per dollar	2.54	2.50"

In the final note for cabinet's approval, the following table is annexed.

Table 3

"TARIFF
11 Tariff has been worked out by Enron on the basis of the following assumptions
— Base load capacity of 625 MW and peaking capacity 70 MW—Phase I
— Total base load capacity of 1905 MW and peaking capacity 110 MW—Phase II
— The availability for the base load is taken at 90% and peaking capacity at 50%
— *import duty of 20% on capital equipment and 15% on LNG and 7% on distillate*
18. The tariff worked out is as under:

Item	Tariff	
	Phase I 1996 Level	Phase II 1998 Level
Capacity charge cents/kWh	3.99	4.39
Energy charge cents/kWh	3.95	3.43
Total charge cents/kWh	7.94	7.82
Rs/kWh at Rs. 32 per dollar	2.54	2.50"

The tariff figure shows discrepancies at different points. At very different levels of customs duty, the tariff remains the same pointing out, both the total lack of application and a desire to push the project through at all costs. Even though the duty on fuel changes from 15 per cent in the first note to 30 per cent and 15 per cent in the second note and finally to 15 per cent and 7 per cent, the tariff remains exactly the same—Rs 2.54 and Rs 2.50 for the first and second phases. Since the total payments to Enron amount to several hundred thousand crore rupees, even a paisa difference in the tariff works out to hundreds of crores. Interestingly, an analysis carried out by the MSEB, which was never given to the government, indicated that the starting tariff would be Rs 3.22! (See Annexure 9)

The "Secret" "Additional" Views of the Finance Department

In September 1993, a Cabinet Note requesting the Cabinet to

allow the MSEB to sign the PPA was finalised. The note which was finally submitted to the cabinet for its approval, for most parts, is innocuous.[45] It does not reveal anything other than some harmless homilies about "the need for the project".

The then Principal Finance Secretary of Maharashtra, Mr Padmanabiah had voiced serious concerns and reservations about various aspects of the project. These reservations of the Department of Finance ought to have been, but were not incorporated in the final cabinet note. A separate "secret" note purporting to be the "additional views of the Finance department", "which remained to be incorporated in the Cabinet Note" was drawn up. These additional views were, however, not presented to the cabinet for its approval.

Considered too unimportant or trivial "to be incorporated" in the final cabinet note, they are as follows:

The department had expressed concern that the "project cost projected" had not been "defined as a ceiling project cost". Therefore, it was "quite possible that in the end, we might end up with cost and time overruns." The department expressed further concern on the issue of costs that "in terms of the agreements that are going to be executed, there does not appear to be any incentive on behalf of Enron to curtail the project cost"; "it would be difficult for us to know exactly what the power is going to cost"; "we cannot but feel that the commitment on behalf of the MSEB is open in absence of the details..."; "Besides, one cannot help feeling that Enron is not taking any risk whatsoever as a generator of power but wants guaranteed rewards, which is not a very satisfactory arrangement."

It went on to say that the cost of LNG was ["extremely

---

[45]The note, inter alia, also observed that "Government guidelines require capital costs to be approved by the CEA".

high"] and was ["not known"], without which the cost of power could not be known. Further, that the project would lead to "*weakening of the credit structure of the MSEB*".[46] It points out that the project "envisages the sale of expensive power to HT industrial users via the MSEB with the profits of such sales being earmarked for payment to Enron on a preferential basis. Incidentally, this amounts roughly to Rs 250 crore per month."

This amount of Rs 250 crore a month was an underestimation by about 30 per cent.[47] In any case, this simply reinforces the Department's conclusion that "...special arrangements made for payment of cost to Enron weakens the residual operations of MSEB, which needs to be serviced by non-HT non-industrial users. This would definitely weaken MSEB and will preclude other MSEB projects from being financed."

The note finally suggests that "the full set of contractual agreements must be received and finalised, not only the Power Purchase Agreement".

None of the points in the note were either brought to the Cabinet's attention nor were they ever considered. The issues raised are valid to date, albeit with greater force.

---

[46]Emphasis in the original.
[47]At the then prevailing exchange rates of Rs. 32 to $ 1.

8

The Public is Informed

The Public is Informed

From the outset, there was no information of any kind available to anyone, right from the CEA, to the project-affected persons and consumers in Maharashtra. All documents quoted were and are still "secret" and "confidential".

The law had mandated the following procedure. The DPC was to prepare a scheme which included revenue details (and therefore tariffs), its financing agreements, the costing of the projects, the need for extra electricity supply and the generation estimate, among other things. Before finalising the scheme and submitting it to the CEA, the proposed scheme was to be notified and advertised to the public. The public was allowed to make representations to the company. A period of two months was allowed by the statute for such representations. The Act specifically provides that the scheme can be submitted to the CEA only after this period of two months and after considering the representations. The CEA was to then evaluate the scheme. Obviously this procedure was found by the DPC to be too onerous and later, almost as an afterthought, the company advertised the scheme one year after finalising it.

In the areas affected by the project there was as yet no inkling of almost anything from the location of the project to its probable consequences. The project was advertised as required under Section 29 of the Electricity Supply Act, 1948 (the 'ESA'). This was the first and perhaps only inkling the public had about the project. On 22 September 1993, the notification was published, as required under Section 29 of the ESA.

Public Notification

In pursuance of the Electricity (Supply) Act, 1948, Dabhol Power Company Unlimited, proposes to take-up the following thermal generation scheme for implementation and accordingly in terms of Section 29 of the said Act, the scheme is hereby published. The salient features of the Scheme is as under:
1. Dabhol Thermal Project (1905 MW Baseload + 110 MW peaking) Total cost: Rs 9,053 crore guaranteed. Fuel: Natural gas (primary fuel), fuel oil (secondary fuel).

This project is envisaged near villages of Veldur, Anjanwel and Dabhol in Ratnagiri district. The plant will be located on the South bank of the Vashishti river as it empties into the Arabian Sea. The project will be completed in about 5 years after approval and commencement of work.

Benefits of the scheme—The energy from the above project shall be supplied to the MSEB for meeting the power demand in the State.

Any licensee or any other person interested in taking objection, if any, in respect of the above scheme may please make representation to that effect within a period of 2 months from the date of publication of this Notification.

Any representation received after 2 months shall not be entertained. The representation or concerned correspondence in this regard, may please be addressed to the Chief Engineer, Dabhol Power Company, "Nirmal" 17th floor, Nariman Point, Bombay 400 021. For any additional information on the above Scheme, please write on the above address.

The meagre information provided in the notification was deficient in material respects. It deliberately misled and misrepresented facts. In particular, it stated that the fuel would be natural gas (not liquefied natural gas), thereby suppressing the fact that fuel would be imported at a very high cost and would involve very heavy capital costs for the port, regassification facilities, etc. This is in fact one of the main reasons why the entire project turned out to be so expensive. It also did not specify that it would be using Distillate No. 2 but mentioned fuel oil (which is substantially cheaper). Further, the notification did not mention other salient features like the cost at which power was to be supplied or that the plant was a base-load plant, etc.

The project had also raised some apprehensions in the minds of the local people. Articles from some widely circulated Marathi papers[48] were the only inkling the local people had about the project and its effect on their lives and land. These reports dealt mainly with the concerns of Bombay based 'environmentalists' about the project's probable polluting effects. They were quite sketchy and offered no real information.

The Letters

The advertisement invited enquiries for additional information. There were a number of queries ranging from requests for consultancy jobs, others requesting details of the acquisition of land to queries about the price of power. The local tehsildar's office[49] had not received any information about the lands proposed to be acquired, despite which, a preliminary survey had already been carried out by the company.

---

[48]Maharashtra Times dated 26/7/93, Maharashtra Times dated 18/8/93, Loksatta dated 15/9/93 and Loksatta dated 21/9/93 for e.g.

[49]Letter from the tehsildar's office to Vinay Nathu, the local MLA dated 14/7/93.

A few (4 letters on record) were from local people offering their services. Shri Nishikant in his letter[50] wrote, to "welcome[51] the venture of your organisation and assure you of the fullest cooperation in all your efforts to start the power station". A local "journalist, editor and proprietor" of the daily *Sagar* and a former Congress MLA from the area for five years, who was then "director" of the MIDC which had "played an important role in the industrial development of Maharashtra", made a suggestion to the DPC, that they "take a positive approach" to various issues of local importance. He assured them of all possible cooperation and welcomed them to the area".

Shri Anna Shriangoamkar, who ran an organisation called "Aparant" suggested that the company should have a local agency "which can effectively tackle" the "many misunderstandings about the project". He offered to "meet company officials" for the same "if they visited the site" or would meet them in Bombay.[52] One Mr Sarang,[53] who introduced himself as a "Retd. Asst. Collector of Customs, Bombay" offered his help in "making applications" and said he would "be glad to work as a consultant" for the company.

However, most (about 80 per cent) of the letters received, were from local people seeking information about the project, its impact and the lands that were to be acquired. The refrain in most of these letters was about the absolute lack of any information of kinds and particularly details about whose lands were to be taken away and the impact of the project on their lives.

---

[50]Shri Nishikant in his letter dated 25/9/93 to the DPC.

[51]The language used is a literal translation from the original Marathi, done by DPC's PR firm. The original translation is retained without any changes despite the errors of language and grammar.

[52]Letter dated November 1 1993 to the DPC.

[53]Letter dated October 1993 to the DPC.

You have published a notice in *Loksatta* dated 21/9/93 and
called upon people to file their objections if any to the project.
I request you to furnish me information about the above
project. Please give me information about population from
the village to be shifted, lands required for the project,
possible pollution (air pollution) from the project, various
advantages and disadvantages to the local people from the
project and the exact area over which the project would be
located. These details would enable the local villagers to form
their opinion about the project...[54]

In the same vein, D.K. Pawar and G.M. Dhopat[55]
requested the DPC to "provide proper compensation" to
people whose lands were being acquired since the lands were
not waste or fallow, they pointed out that the local people
should get priority in employment; and that the company
should give a guarantee that the project would not have an
adverse effect on agriculture, horticulture, animal and human
life in the area.

Specific objections were voiced in a letter from D.K. Pawar
who refused to "give [his] lands for this project". He had
already registered his objections with the tehsildar of the
village. A copy of the letter written to the tehilsadar as well
as other objections were sent to the DPC. He further
requested the DPC to issue a "proper clarification about all
the issues involved".

There were a few letters from local inhabitants requesting
further information and telling the company to stop
destroying their fields and orchards in the course of the
preliminary survey

M/s AFCONS carried out some demolishment of a 10 feet

---

[54]Letter dated 22/9/93 from Shri Bhuvad to the Chief Engineer, DPC.
[55]D.K. Pawar and G.M. Dhopat in their letter to the DPC dated
6/20/93.

canal well and did some boring work. They left without completing their work, in the process causing damage to my 185 grafting and 90 cashew trees.[56]

Some people complained that the company had "been resorting to activities like cutting trees, making roads etc. without the prior permission of the concerned land holders" and the company was requested to take cognizance of the same failing which "the people will start an agitation".[57]

Two letters in particular were from people outside the area. One was from the Mumbai Grahak Panchayat,[58] a consumer organisation, and the other from Swadeshi Jagran Manch, a front organisation of the RSS. Both requested specific information from the company.

The letter from the Mumbai Grahak Panchayat stated that it was a "Registered Voluntary Consumer Organisation" and was "concerned" since it "directly affects the consumers in Maharashtra". They stated that the "notification issued" was "bad in law" since the "Dabhol Power Company Unlimited" was neither a "board" nor a "generating company" as defined under the ESA. Therefore, the DPC was "neither empowered to invite objections to the scheme nor competent to consider such objections". The entire process itself was therefore, "null and void".

"Without prejudice to the above" they went on to state that "the details furnished in the Public Notification" were "inadequate" and therefore requested the DPC to furnish them again. The details that were requested included the "detailed scheme for Dabhol Thermal Project": the "total cost

---

[56]Letter from Mrs. Pratibha Pravin Vaidya, a affected owner, dated 23/9/93 to the Chief Engineer, DPC.

[57]Letter dated 25/10/93 from P.K. Dali to the DPC on behalf of a local committee of concerned citizens.

[58]Representation dated 18/11/93 from Mumbai Grahak Panchayat to DPC.

involved, profits envisaged, and the price structure", the company's sources of "funds" and whether the "total cost of Rs 9,053 crore mentioned in the Notification" included the cost of harbour development. They also requested the DPC to send them "technical literature" on the project.

The Response

These and other requests from the local people seem very reasonable. The DPC made no attempt to allay any misgivings or provide any information at all. A form letter was sent out to most people, telling them all their concerns would be looked into.

In response to specific queries about the project's impact, the land to be acquired, etc., DPC's response in the form letter was to lie to the people by simply stating that nothing was really known and that there would be no adverse impact on the area.

"The final location and the exact area required is in the process of being determined and after finalisation, a notification giving the survey number and GAT number will be issued to this effect. Rehabilitation, if necessary will be done in accordance with the State Policy of the Government of Maharashtra."

This was obviously not true, since the company had known the exact location of the station for the past two years. They went on to simply claim that everything would be determined by the government.[59]

---

[59]"Land rates will be determined by the Land Acquisition Officer under the provisions of the Land Acquisition Act; Valuation of fruit bearing trees, if any, will be undertaken as per the decision of the officials of the Horticulture Department; Valuation of structures, if any, will be in accordance with the assessment made by the PWD/MIDC engineers Fuel wood and timber trees, if any, will be assessed as per the valuation by the Forest Department officials".

They refused to give any information requested by the Mumbai Grahak Panchayat, and the Swadeshi Jagaran Manch. The DPC went on to say that the information requested was "being thoroughly looked at by several competent authorities including the Government of Maharashtra, the Central Electricity Authority (CEA), the Foreign Investment Promotion Board (FIPB) and the Cabinet Committee for Economic Affairs (CCEA)". They asked them to appreciate that as the DPC was a "generating company whose sole customer is the MSEB, any tariff related questions which affect consumers must be directly related to MSEB".

Compliance with Section 29

On 22 November, the two-month period under Section 29 expired. All requests for information including details regarding cost of electricity, capital costs, etc. were refused. On 23 November 1993, the day after the last date given in the public notification, the MSEB wrote to the CEA,[60] stating that the "power purchase agreement, cost details etc. cannot be given to the representationists until the project is cleared". Till date, i.e., 1998, no one has any indication of the price of electricity.

Interestingly enough, on 21 November 1993, the day before the last date on which objections were to be received, the DPC wrote a letter[61] to the CEA reporting "compliance of Section 29". They also wrote to the GoM that they had received no objections.

On 23 November 1993, the GoM wrote to the CEA, stating "M/s Enron have stated that they have not received any objections" on the "proposed Dabhol power project". Therefore, "the requirements of Section 29" of the ESA "have been met".

---

[60]Letter dated 23/11/93 from the MSEB to the CEA.
[61]Letter dated 21/11/93 from DPC to the CEA.

However, the CEA appears to have independently learnt that at least 34 representations were received by the company. It faxed a letter to the GoM, stating that "it has been reported that 34 respondents have been received". It went on to ask whether "Section 29" of the Act was complied with.

On 24 November, the GoM (realising that the CEA was aware of representations), changed its mind and "had a look at all the responses" that the DPC received. The government stated that the DPC had "replied to 37 of those responses". The GoM had a "look at the replies given by the DPC" and found the DPC's replies to be "adequate". It "specifically looked into the two applications" mentioned in your fax message that is those of Mumbai Grahak Panchayat and Swadeshi Jagaran Manch.

The GoM claimed that these bodies had "raised broad issues concerning the project, like the technical details, capital structure of the policy, tariff issues and the broad policy issues of the Central and the State Government". It went on to state that these issues had been "looked into by agencies like CEA, Department of Power, Ministry of Finance, FIPB, CCEA and, of course, the Government of Maharashtra/MSEB", and therefore felt, that "the action desired to be taken under Section 29" of the ESA had "been duly taken and complied with by the DPC".

Land Acquisition

Under the Maharashtra Industrial Development Act, 1961, the acquisition of land is done by the Maharashtra Industrial Development Corporation (MIDC). The conditions for compulsory acquisition are completely arbitrary. The Act states, under the heading of Acquisition: "If, at any time in the opinion of the State Government, any land is required for the purpose of development by the Corporation...the State Government may acquire such land by publishing in the Official Gazette a notice..." There is no obligation to choose land that will affect the least number of people or which will do minimal damage to agriculture or the environment. Any land can be acquired by the mere publication of a notice.

The acquisition procedures make it very difficult for the affected people to object. The Act continues, "After considering such cause, if any, shown by the owner of the land and by any other person interested therein and after giving such owner and person an opportunity of being heard the State Government may pass such orders as it deems fit". There are no specific reasons given as to why the owners can resist acquisition. All that is available to the evicted is "an opportunity of being heard", not necessarily answered. In the Dabhol case, the objections of the occupants were given in writing but no answers were ever given, written or oral, in contravention of the Act. The act further specifies that "If any person refuses or fails to comply with an order made under Section (5) (to surrender possession to the Government), the State Government may take possession of the land, and may for that purpose use such force as may be necessary." The Act does not provide for any resettlement.

Judicial Review

A writ petition filed in the Bombay High Court in April 1994 by those who received acquisition notices, challenging the legality of the acts and the procedures for acquisition, was summarily thrown out in July 1994. The judicial bench said that the peititoners were not entitled to resettlement according to current laws, which make resettlement compulsory only for large irrigation projects.

One might recollect the objections under Section 28/29 that were filed by the local people. However, during the course of the petition, in his affidavit, Frost Cochran, Director of the DPC swore that the petitioners should have objected when the notice regarding the Enron Project was gazetted by the Maharashtra government in September 1993. He also stated that the government had organised meetings to explain the project to the people. In addition to their Section 28/29 objections, the local people had raised objections to the project in a memorandum submitted to the DPC on 6 November, 1993. The DPC did not deign to reply or consider either.

Additionally, one might recollect that the representations were to be received till 22 November, 1993. However, Ajit Nimbalkar, of the MSEB, revealed in his affidavit: that "On 14 September 1993 the Chief Minister...said that preliminary work would start by December, 1993". The Chief Minister was either prescient or was sure that all objections would be overruled within a few days.

9

The Environmental Aspects

At the outset, I would like to make it clear that the environmental case per se against the project is relatively weak. However, the manner in which the clearances were obtained, in violation of law and in travesty of norms, is of particular concern.

Given the 'fact' that power plants are being set up and will continue to be set up, a very strong case can be made that in this particular case, the choice of fuel and the location are certainly not in the best interests of the country, the state and the region. Consider the first aspect: that of the choice of fuel. Natural gas is less polluting than coal. However, 'standard' technology enables coal to be nearly as 'benign' as gas particularly in terms of emissions of SO_x. However, in terms of the gross amount of CO_2 produced, 1 kg of coal produces more CO_2 than gas and the problems of ash disposal remain.

In 1993, around the same time that the Enron PPA was being negotiated, the company was also trying to obtain enormous reserves of gas and oil off the western coast of India about 350 km north of Dabhol. The government, in its infinite wisdom, chose to hand the fields to Enron for a song. Enron obtained these fields and the company is producing gas from there. This gas which could have been used for power plants, preferably peaking, is being sold to the government. The payment is in foreign exchange. The company is being paid US $ 2.97 to US $ 3.11/MMBTU of gas. This is about fifty per cent more than the price received by Enron in the USA and 230 per cent more than its fields in the West Indies. Interestingly enough, we will be paying the same company considerably more (about US $ 4.5 per MMBTU), in the form of gas imports for the Dabhol power plant. The loss in purely economic terms amounts to a few billion dollars on this count alone. This is dealt with at greater length in Annexure 1.

Background

The plant was sought to be located by Enron at Dabhol, about 260 km south of Bombay on the Konkan coast. Existing guidelines for the siting of thermal power plants would have precluded this in the first place, given the ecologically fragile nature of the region. The project is located on the estuary of the Vashishti river that supports diverse biological life forms including some protected species of flora and fauna. The project lies in a fault area prone to earthquakes and has experienced tremors as late as in April 1996.

The project has, since the various original clearances, been substantially modified. The original project was for a 695 MW plant with a 1320 MW second phase which was not binding. It has since been expanded into a 2184 MW plant, the Power Purchase agreement for which had been signed only in late 1996. It is substantially different from the earlier project, about three times bigger than the one for which various clearances, including the water clearance were obtained. The first phase fuel was changed from distillate no. 2 to naphtha. No environmental assessments appear to have been carried out for naphtha.

Breaches of Law

The statutorily binding and standard environmental guidelines for thermal power plants were observed more in the breach:

The siting criteria requirements were breached. The requirement of a 5 km buffer zone between the High Tide Line and the plant was flagrantly breached (Clause 2.2.2). The project is located near mangroves, and the construction jetty directly faces the mangroves on the other side of the estuary within 500 metres of the jetty; the project is near Anjanvel fort (breaches of clauses 2.2.1, and 2.2.6). Further, no rehabilitation plant was made (clause 3.4 and 4.3.1). Disaster Management Plans were not drawn up and/or were not drawn up adequately. In particular, no serious note was taken of the fact of storage of huge quantities of inflammable material in a seismic zone. All clearances were obtained by the inadequate disclosure of facts or by misrepresenting facts.

The Ministry of Environment and Forests (MoEF) requires that each project promoter submits Environmental Impact Assessment (EIA) reports. Initially a Rapid EIA can be submitted on which the MoEF gives conditional clearance, but a Comprehensive EIA is required for final clearance. Enron submitted its Rapid EIA report to the MoEF in June 1993 and provisional clearance had been granted on that basis. The Comprehensive Report was submitted to the MoEF in June 1994.

The DPC claims that the EIA report is a confidential document, not to be made available to the public, including the people living near the project site. This is astonishing, since every project must have an impact on the local people who are an integral part of the environment. The DPC in a reply insisted that "The Environmental Impact Assessment report is a document that we, are not at liberty to circulate".[62]

The MoEF clearances are given on the assumption that the data in the EIA report is correct and complete. The EIA claims that the data on which it is based "was obtained by site visits, discussion with local officials and with a few selected people of the area". The persons in the site area, however, emphatically assert that not a single one of them was asked any questions by Enron's consultants. The EIA report states that the land to be acquired is "wasteland", "unused land", "not very productive and that people grew only one rain *kharif* crop of paddy, *ragi* (*Eleusine coracana*) or *wari* (*Panicum milliaceum*)". The horticulture is said to be "poor". "The vegetation on the project site is scrubby and sparse because of the rocky soil...".

Local farmers, however, insist that about 50 per cent of the land to be acquired is under crop cultivation, 5 per cent under horticulture, 10 per cent kept for pasture and 35 per cent under private forests. They cultivate 13 cereal, pulse and oilseed crops, often more than one a year, with good yields. They also grow 17 species of fruit trees.

In their "Report on a Field Visit to Dabhol", on 19 February 1994, submitted by three members of the Environmental Assessment Committee (EAC), the committee stated that:

> ...as we proceeded along the route to the jetty site, several groups of local residents submitted memoranda to Mr Khambog, detailing their objections to the Enron project...To begin with, we discovered that local communities were unaware of the DPC plans till very recently. It was, for instance, only three days before we arrived that the first notices for land acquisition were received by

---

[62]Letter from DPC to the Mumbai Grahak Panchayat.

villagers. This has caused considerable discontent among the villagers and though our itinerary was not public knowledge we were stopped at least eight times along the route by people protesting the siting of large-scale projects in and around their lands.

That the whole process of obtaining environmental clearances has been turned into a farce is shown by the remarks of the EAC members in the same report:

> We might mention that as we were setting off for Dabhol from Chiplun we were informed by Mr Iyer that the Ministry of Environment had accorded environmental clearance to the thermal plant of Dabhol Power Company. This came as a surprise as we felt that it would have been in order for the Ministry to obtain our committee's report before communicating any approval to the project authorities. We make this point because it is obvious that the project would be unworkable at the present site if, perchance, the jetty site is found unsuitable.

The High Court Order

An environmental group, SOCLEEN challenged the clearances in the Mumbai High Court, which was disposed off by consent order. The consent terms agreed to in the SOCLEEN writ petition, included the setting up of an expert committee. This committee was ordered to conduct a review and supplementary appraisal of the Dabhol Thermal Power plant, the jetty and the fuel facilities. The Dabhol Power Company (DPC) agreed to furnish all the relevant documents and information which were not supplied earlier to the central government. The Court set a definite schedule. The committee was to meet within two weeks of the signing of the consent terms and submit its report within another two weeks. The terms had specified that "the Summary of (the) report and recommendations of the expert committee...be available at the office of...(MoEF) at Bombay to the petitioners, other environmental groups and others... on request by a date to be specified..." Thereafter, there would be hearings at which MoEF officials would consider the objections of the public.

The Expert Committee

While the committee duly met and heard the issues from the the DPC, the MSEB and the Government of Maharashtra, it did not hear from the project-affected people or from others concerned about the project. No provision was made for the latter's attendance in the court order.

The Inspection Process

The Summary was prepared and the MoEF proposed to display it at Delhi, at a distance of 1200 km from the project site, despite the court specifying that it should be displayed in Bombay. After objections were raised, the MoEF shifted the location to Bombay, but introduced several other hurdles. The documents were displayed in the MoEF office at the Cargo Complex of the Sahar International Airport, on 31 October 1994. Copies of the summary of the Expert Committee report were laid out. No photocopying was allowed and no copy was permitted to be taken out of the building.

The Summary of the Documents Submitted by DPC

The Summary of the DPC documents is complacent, bland, and completely untroubled by any doubt that the project may be delayed. The whole attitude was redolent of a foregone conclusion. The Summary did not fulfill the intent of the court order. It did have not supply information which would allowed the local people and environmentalists to estimate the impact of the project. Of the few facts which are given, several are false and self-contradictory. The document is filled with deliberately omitted information and abounds in internally inconsistent and self-contradictory statements. It contains factual errors, particularly on environmental matters. Pertinent facts regarding technical matters are concealed, others are distorted to show the project in a better light. A detailed analysis of these and other related issues has been set out in some detail in various issues of the *Indranet Journal.*[63]

A detailed analysis is given in Indranet. However a few typical examples would suffice.

a. False and Misleading Statements

It is stated in the Summary, that "Along the estuary there are a few mangrove patches". In reality there are about 20 acres of mangroves existing in the estuary up to 3 km from the construction jetty site. It is said that "There are no reports with the forest department of any endangered or protected species of flora and fauna in the region". The Red Data Book of Indian Plants (published by the Botanical Survey of India, in three volumes) lists two endangered and ten rare species of plants in the district.

b. Technical Incompetence

The document states that "Prevailing winds during the summer and winter months are typically NE at two to seven (2–7) km/hr. During the monsoon season, these winds typically shift NW, averaging seven to fourteen (7–14) km/hr."[30] The winds do not "typically shift NW", they always shift SW. Such elementary errors are surprising. There is no point in mentioning average wind values. Monsoon squalls can suddenly reach speeds of more than 60 km/hr.

Another statement is as follows "The dredged material from the construction jetty will be 3.9 million cubic metres,

---

[63]Indranet Journal published from 79, Carter Road, Bandra (W), Bombay 400 050. The data here is from various issues between 1993 and 1995 authored by Winin Pereira, Abhay Mehta, Mangesh Chavan and Subash Sule.

plus another 2 million cubic metres for the LNG jetty". The disposal of the dredged material "will be in the sea, approximately 8 km west of the shore at water of depth 20 m CD". Neither the disposal areas nor the dredged areas are particularly productive for marine life, hence, even though some short term disruption of the ecosystems will occur because of dredging activities, the losses are not significant. However, no data has been given to support such assertions. It has been recommended that the dredged material be spread over a large area. A total of about 6 million cubic meters spread over 6 million square metres (600 hectares) will form a layer 1 metre thick, effectively killing all benthic organisms.

The Public Hearings

The public hearings were held at Sachivalaya in Bombay on the 8 and 9 November 1994. Since the documents that were ordered to be displayed were not made available, the chairman was requested to either postpone the hearings or have an additional hearing after making the relevant documents available and before taking a final decision on the subject. This request was turned down. On 8 November, 1994, a large crowd of people who claimed to have come all the way from Guhagar, demanded to be heard. They were given priority, although there were several people who had arrived earlier. They claimed that the project was a good one and that they wanted it to proceed. It turned out that none of them were from the affected region, but were simply people that had been hired by the DPC, and brought to Bombay in buses. They were received by officials of the DPC at the venue of the hearings.

When the Guhagar people finished, several NGOs spoke, all objecting to the project on grounds of environmental damage, lack of information provided by the DPC, the need for such expensive power, the cost of the project and so on.

The following memoranda were submitted by the local people:

1. Yeshwant Sonu Bait and 368 others from the project-affected villages:

"The Government of Maharashtra declared in the Marathi daily...At that time the local residents did not have detailed information about the project...that local residents would be deprived of their present reasonable and comfortable life and they will all be ruined. As against this, information given by the Company and the Government was more or less creating confusion in the minds of the people. In this respect a number of letters were sent to the concerned departments of the government but no replies have been received..."

...that certain facts about the project are not revealed. The exact land required for the project is not known. It is stated to be 450 hectares, sometimes 550 hectares, and on some other occasions 700 hectares. Notices sent for acquisition relate to 607 hectares. While acquiring land the boundary of the land being acquired is so demarcated that the residential clusters are excluded from acquisition. At some places land on three sides of a residential cluster is acquired...clearly to show that no residential house is being acquired. This creates a doubt about the real intention of the government and the DPC. The land under acquisition includes horticultural land, paddy land, land on which crops like nagli and wari are taken, grass lands and lands which provide fuel wood.

"The landholders gave their objections in reply to each of the notices received by them regarding acquisition of their land and all these difficulties were explained including the difficulties of possible pollution from the project but government has not responded at all. Out of 607 hectares, about 25 per cent land has been handed over to the government and the remaining 75 per cent land has not been handed over and shall not be handed over by the cultivators. Those who handed over land to the government did so under various types of threats and not voluntarily. The fifth notice was given to those who had not handed over land voluntarily and the date fixed for taking possession by panchanama was 16th August (1994), but no panchanama was taken on that day. Thereafter, on 20th September, another notice regarding taking possession by force by drawing a panchanama was published at conspicuous public places and on 21st September the Tehsildar, the Sub-divisional Officer, the Land acquisition officer, two panchas from outside the village and the police patil came to the village and instead of going to each parcel of land, they came to the main village square for just ten minutes, obtained signatures of the police patil and two panchas brought from outside, with the actual panchanama on the land itself never done..."

..."The exact site of the jetties to be constructed is not being shown. The location from where cooling water will be drawn and the point at which it will be released are also not indicated." The employment potential of Rs 9000 crore Dabhol Project is extremely limited and whatever few jobs that are available will not be given to the local people because they would not be fit for such jobs...

"We shall not give land for the project and if any force is used we have to resist it at the cost of our lives. If government wants to use force we are ready for it, but we shall not allow the project to be established here. This may please be noted and the project may please be canceled."

2. The Vidyut Prakalp Dakshata Committee Veldur, Taluka Guhagar, signed by 113 residents:

"We, the residents of village Veldur, hereby represent to you that we have strong objection to the Dabhol Power Project that is being set up in the villages of Veldur, Anjanwel and Ranvi in Guhagar Taluka in Ratnagiri district."

"While various actions to set up this project were in progress, we the local people were kept in the dark by the Government, and the project authorities and the project is being imposed on us... The memorandum then goes on to elaborate on the effects of the plant's pollution and the jetties on their agriculture and fishing. They then state that...It is therefore requested that...the project should not be given clearance."

3. The Konkan Sangharsh Samiti:

"We wish to bring to your kind notice that we strongly oppose the Enron power project or any other polluting project which aims to strike at the foundations of the local economy."

"We object to Enron on the following grounds:" The company or the government has not made available project reports, EIA (Environmental Impact Assessment) reports or power purchase agreement in spite of our demand for it persistently made during last one and half years. This creates doubts about their intention. We feel that many of these documents must have been prepared either on false information or on half truths.

"In the development plan of Ratnagiri district there is no reservation made for any specific area for locating chemical industries or huge projects like Enron. In spite of this, disregarding the development plan, these projects are imposed on the people." (Several other grounds for opposing the project are given.)

"We request you to consider the above reasons on a scientific basis and to give us justice. Kindly help us to stop the encroachment on our region by projects like Enron and others which would come up because of Enron."

4. V.S. Vaidya and 64 other residents of Anjanvel village:

"The Enron Power Project is being established in our village. We fear that after this project is established, the air in our village will be polluted and our life would be ruined...We feel that the project will affect horticulture and ruin our main source of livelihood..."

5. Dr V.P. Sakpal and 91 other persons of Mouze Deoghar, Zombadi, Taluka Guhagar:

"We oppose this project which is striking at the very root of our life. Due to the increase in the cost of power, village industries and agriculture would suffer.

The government and big industrialists are imposing these projects on us without making available sufficient data about their projects and without informing us about the damage they would cause."

6. 73 Residents of Shringartali, Janavle, Velamb, Chikhale, Parchuri, Malan, Guhagar, Koundar:

Several grounds for opposing the project are given... "We therefore demand: 'take away Enron project and save the country and save Konkan'."

7. Gajanan D. Relekar, Municipal Councillor, and 17 other residents of Chiplun:

"The Maharashtra Industrial Development Corporation, the State Government and the concerned industries were repeatedly requested by us (for information) about pollution but they deliberately turned a deaf ear to our prayers and that is why we were forced to go to the court." The Regional Development Plan has been completely disregarded...

"There is a ruthless effort through the governmental agencies to push this project through by making unlimited use of the power vested in government, false propaganda and by taking undue advantage of the mild nature of poor land holders and their helplessness."

8. Dr Ninay Natu, President, Guhagar, Chiplun, Dapoli Parisar Bachav Sangharsh Samiti, also signed by the Sarpanch, Shri Chandrashekhar Bhave and 45 other residents of Guhagar:

..."we do not have any reliable information..."

An Orchestrated Farce

Further evidence that the procedure was merely an orchestrated farce is revealed in the words of Robert Bakley, president of the DPC. He told members of the Indo-American Chamber of Commerce, North India Council on 17 November, 1994, that the construction of the first phase would commence before January 1995 and that the environment clearance for the second phase of the project was "likely early next week". One might recollect that the public hearing was on 9 November.

On 24 November the final clearances were promptly issued by the MoEF. It was the DPC and not the MoEF who issued a report to this effect which appeared in the press on 25 November. All objections raised by members of the Expert Committee and the NGOs at the public hearings were totally ignored.

The Revised EIA

Certain clearances obtained by DPC on 16 February 1994 and 12 March 1994 were to merge in the final orders to be passed by the Central Government. The comprehensive EIA that was prepared thereafter carefully conceals substantial and relevant details which are material to any decision on granting environmental clearances. In the comprehensive EIA, there is absolutely no document or mention anywhere of DPC's intention of quarrying, to cut the hill which leads into the waterfront in the estuary that lies within the exclusion zone of 500 metres under the Coastal Regulation Zone. Additionally, there is no mention anywhere of the intention to reclaim land (or land fill, as DPC euphemistically calls it). Consequently, nobody knew that these activities would take place until they actually occurred. Even the comprehensive EIA has no mention of them. The MoEF clearances were in breach of existing guidelines, and were obtained through suppression of material fact and include activities which are banned by the CRZ notifications.

The deliberate suppression of information and the supply of false information, in themselves should have vitiated the clearances, as per the law. However, no such event has occurred.

10

The Power Purchase Agreement

The Power Purchase Agreement

The PPA, signed between the MSEB and the DPC on 8 December 1993, is remarkable in its complexity. It obfuscates seemingly trivial issues to such an extent that perhaps there is no single person or organisation who can understand all aspects—legal, technical and economic—of the document.

This includes the GoM and the MSEB whose vacuity of understanding, both deliberate and real, has been amply demonstrated in earlier chapters. Dr Harne, formerly of the MSEB, seems to have been the only person competent enough to make sense of some of the technical complexities. The entire document is a challenge to any organisation in the country. This includes the GoM and all its departments, the MSEB and the entire GoI. The only redeeming feature of the agreement as then signed, was that phase 2 of the project was completely optional and non-binding upon the MSEB.

The agreement between the MSEB and the DPC specified that the company would build, operate and sell electricity in the form of available capacity. Additional payments for fuel on a take or pay basis make the MSEB pay for all the contracted fuel. Effectively this implies that the total payments are fixed and nearly independent of the amount of electricity drawn by the MSEB. Additional payments were to be made if the turbine was turned on or if the plant capacity was tested.

Under the PPA, the tariff is based on two parts: capacity charge and the charge for fuel. The capacity charge includes:

— a capital recovery charge: capital, debt service and equity return;

— fixed O&M (operation and maintenance);

— tax incremental charges.

Capital Cost

There was no mention anywhere in the PPA of the capital expenditure on the plant. The officially advertised cost was Rs 9053 crore (about US $ 2,830 million) as compared with a cost of US $ 1,200 million for a similar plant that Enron built in England. (The 1875 MW Teesside power station). The capital cost per MW is US $ 1.40 million for Dabhol, compared with US $ 0.64 million for Teesside, making Dabhol 2.2 times as expensive as Teesside.

The capital cost is not the ceiling cost. Costs could and have increased since there is no cap on capital expenditure: (Clause. 13.1 read with Clause. 13.6 and Clause. 16 of the PPA.)

Capacity Charges

The PPA has over 6 pages of complex interlinked formulae to calculate capacity charges. It does not state the capital recovery charge,[64] particularly in the assumptions used in

---

[64]Although West Merchant Bank and the CEA did some kind of an exercise in calculating it.

arriving at the critical 'constant' used in the formulae for the payment of the capacity charges. The variables in calculating the capital recovery charge include the dollar to rupee ratio, the rate of Indian inflation, the rate of inflation in the USA, the US labour inflation index, and the US materials inflation index. It may be noted that between 1993 and 1998, on account of a single variable—the dollar to rupee valuation—capacity charges have increased by nearly 40 per cent.

It is to be appreciated that all payments are in bulk, i.e., if the MSEB, as may very well be the case, picks up, say, half the contracted capacity, the total payments would still be the same, effectively making the cost per unit double.

Violations of Law

The PPA ignores, circumvents and/or violates the Electricity Supply Act, 1948 E(S)A, which is the governing act for the supply of electricity in India. The three statutory bodies constituted under the aegis of the E(S)A in respect of any power project are the CEA, the MSEB and the State Electricity Consultative Council (SECC). The CEA has already been dealt with earlier.

Of these, the SECC is a statutory body constituted under Section 16 of the E(S)A. This section makes it mandatory for state governments to institute such a body by stating that "the State Government shall constitute an SECC for the state." One of the functions of the SECC was to advise the board (i.e. the MSEB) and the generating company (the DPC in this case) on questions of policy and major schemes. Maharashtra is supposed to have had one such SECC, but it had lapsed in 1991. The state government did nothing to revive it. The matter was even referred to the court which ordered the state government on 6 June 1993 to reconstitute/revive the SECC within six months of the order (by 6 December, 1993). But it was not revived until January/ February 1995, well after the PPA was signed on 8 December, 1993. Hence, there was no mandatory statutory body in existence at the time when the PPA was signed.

There are clauses in the PPA which make a mockery of the powers vested with the MSEB. For instance, one clause in the PPA clearly states that

> The parties hereby agree that any exercise by MSEB of its statutory powers to require DPC to perform the duties of generating companies set out in Section 18 Article 1 of the E(S)A...or any exercise of MSEB under Section 55 of the said act...shall be deemed to be a change in law.

The MSEB has virtually surrendered all rights, including that of inspecting the power station and fuel tanks (MSEB is paying for the fuel), and even the right to enter the station. As per the PPA, only "duly authorised" MSEB personnel "who have been approved by the DPC in advance" can enter the station, on 'two occasions in any one month, upon a notice of 'no less than two hours'.

Section 18(I) of the E(S)A requires 'Generating companies to establish substations and main transmission lines', as may be required by the competent authority. The PPA made it a precondition for the MSEB to build, at its own cost, the 400 KV line(s) for the transmission of electricity from the plant site to load centres. According to the Auditor General's report, the cost to the MSEB was estimated to be around Rs 322 crore. (This is for the first phase.)

Section 55 of the E(S)A states that every generating company should follow the directions of the Board (the MSEB in this case) and the regional grid boards to ensure integrated grid operations. But this according to the PPA could be construed as a change in law by the DPC.

Under the agreement it is nearly impossible for the MSEB

to terminate the agreement though the DPC has been granted almost unilateral freedom to do so.

Specific Exemptions

The PPA also exempts the DPC from the payment of any sales tax or duties on the electricity sought to be generated and sold by it. This is an exception to Section 3 of the Bombay Electricity Duty Act 1958. The DPC has also obtained exemption from the Maharashtra Sales of Electricity Act 1963. In addition, the DPC has managed to wrest concessions in respect of income tax provisions as well. For instance, it has managed an exemption from the provisions of Section 10(15) of the Income Tax Act which relate to interest payable by the DPC on offshore debt. A similar instance is the exemption from the provisions of Section 10(6) which relates to the tax on payments by the DPC to its non-resident contractor. The DPC had also been granted an income tax holiday through 1998, which was extendable. It has also obtained exemption from the provisions of the Bombay Stamp Act. It does not have to pay anything to the government as required under Section 9(1) on amounts secured by mortgage deeds.

This is indeed surprising because all other companies including private and electricity companies like the Tata Electrical Companies are liable and do in fact pay these taxes in the course of normal business operations.

No Guarantee Against Delay in Construction

If there is a delay in plant construction, the DPC pays nothing from its pocket, neither as interest on loans nor as penalties to the MSEB. The DPC is said to be liable for stringent penalties[65] in case of non-performance such as time

---

[65]Most of the data that follows is taken from Prayas's report.

over-run, capacity short fall, etc. The DPC passes on most of these penalties to its contractors. It is not likely to pay anything from its pocket and in some cases (of non-performance) even earns profits. One of the main planks of the pro-Enron argument was a set of various performance guarantees from the DPC and the related penalties it has agreed to pay in case of default.

However, the actual case is as follows.

Parameter	DPC pays MSEB	Contractors pay DPC
1. Delay in construction		
a) Upto six months	U$ 14,000/day	U$ 250,000/day
b) After six months	U$ 110,000/day	U$ 340,000/day
2. Shortfall in capacity	U$ 100/kW	U$ 1,892/kW

This means that the DPC makes considerably more money than the fines it pays the MSEB in case of a delay. Effectively, the DPC will retain nearly US $ 230,000 per day after paying a penalty to the MSEB. This is enough to meet the daily interest payment on all debt and allows an additional margin of Rs 13 lakhs a day for other expenses.

Between the DPC and the MSEB, the plant will be considered commissioned only if it can operate at a minimum of 80 per cent of the nominal capacity.[66] If the contractor fails to deliver 725 MW, DPC would get U$ 1,892 per kW of capacity shortage.

However, the DPC pays only US $ 100 per kW as penalty to the MSEB (for shortfall below 695 MW). This means that the DPC earns Rs 6 crore per MW of the shortfall (below 725) but pays the MSEB only Rs 0.32 crore/MW of shortfall below 695.

GE has guaranteed the DPC a maximum heat rate of 7,460 Btu/kWh, called the guaranteed heat rate, i.e. an efficiency of 45.7 per cent. If the heat rate exceeds this, the contractor will

---

[66]i.e. 80% of 695 MW = 556 MW.

pay the DPC US $ 121,000 per Btu/kWh of the increase. The DPC, in turn has promised the MSEB a heat rate of 7605 i.e. 145 Btu/kWh higher than what GE has promised. If the heat rate is lower than 7605, then the DPC gets a bonus. For a base load capacity of 625 MW, a maximum heat rate of 7605[67] will be considered for payments to the DPC. If the operating heat rate is lower, the DPC will not pass the full benefit to the MSEB. 25 per cent of the difference will be passed on to the DPC as bonus.

Interestingly enough, even the much higher heat rate is not "guaranteed". If after some years of use, the plant efficiency drops and the heat rate increases, the PPA mandates that this is to be treated as a "change in costs". All changes in costs will be borne by the MSEB.

Additional Charges

There are additional charges that all users would be paying for the use of port facilities. The port/harbour/regassification facility will be paid for by consumers as part of capital costs. Enron will however use each of these facilities for private profit: one third of port revenues and all revenues from the sale of gas to other commercial users accrue to Enron.

In addition to the above charges, the MSEB pays fees to the DPC for some special operations. These include:

(i) a fuel management fee of US $ 2.5 million per year, increasing at the US rate of inflation.

(ii) a fee in case the MSEB unnecessarily undertakes the capacity test. If the DPC proves that the capacity test was not needed, the MSEB pays US $ 50,000.

(iii) a fee for hot and cold starts. The hot start fees (applicable for a shutdown of less than 12 hours) are

---

[67]i.e. a minimum efficiency of 44.9%.

US $ 10,429 for 9FAGT and US $ 5,015 for steam turbine.

The Secrecy

The PPA was treated as a top 'secret' document. All attempts to secure a copy of the agreement were rebuffed by the DPC as well as the MSEB. To illustrate, the Mumbai Grahak Panchayat, a consumer organisation, requested the MSEB and the DPC for a copy of the PPA.

This request was refused and the MSEB claimed that the PPA was a "confidential document", while the DPC said that it was a "sensitive" agreement. In its reply the DPC stated that

> *To a country as yet unused to the phenomenon of privatisation this may be difficult to understand, but in a competitive market a power purchase agreement (PPA) is the one document that affords companies an edge over the other players in the field. It represents the skills of each of the arms of the company—finance, engineering and law to produce a deal that can win a contract for a company. You will therefore appreciate the fact that such a document is zealously guarded by all companies.*

The question of competition does not arise, since the DPC did not bid for the contract and all its output was being purchased by one customer, the MSEB.

11

The Guarantees

The purchase of electricity by the MSEB and the payments due therefrom are governed by various agreements. These include the PPA, the Guarantee by the state of Maharashtra, the State Support Agreement, the Counter Guarantee by the Union of India and the tripartite agreement between the GoM, the GoI and the Reserve Bank of India.

These terms for the purchase of electricity by a utility are unprecedented. Under the terms of the PPA, the MSEB has promised to pay for the purchase of electricity and/or electrical generating capacity and/or fuel. The payments are to be made on the basis of availability and the DPC is to be paid about 1,380 crore in the first year of the first phase (at the then prevailing exchange rates and oil prices). At current rates, the first bill amounted to Rs 135 crores plus an additional 100 crores as taking and other charges. This amounts to at least Rs 1600 crores a year. Payments for the second phase start at US $ 1323 million every year (about Rs 4,700 crores then, Rs 5,600 crores currently).

If the MSEB cannot for some reason pay, or there are delays in paying these dues, the DPC's first recourse is the irrevocable letter of credit that the MSEB is supposed to open in the DPC's favour. This is against the MSEB's receivables, i.e., most payments that the MSEB receives or will receive from its overall sales are pledged in making the payments to the DPC.

In the event of the MSEB failing to make the payments, the guarantee signed by the GoM promises to irrevocably and unconditionally guarantee to pay to the DPC any and every sum of money which the MSEB is liable to pay under the PPA. Under the terms of the counter guarantee, the Republic of India counter guarantees the payments due to the DPC in the event of a GoM default. The GoI is also liable for a part of the payments due to the DPC under the PPA. In this event, the GoI will ask the RBI to directly deduct the amount from the constitutionally sanctioned share of revenues due to the state of Maharashtra.

The Total Exposure

This is not a one-time obligation. It recurs every year. 'Normal guarantees' are limited to, at best, the total exposure on the total amounts of loans raised. In this case, by guaranteeing all and any payments for the term of the entire agreement, the GoM has de facto guaranteed everything.

In particular, concern is directed at the absolute magnitude of the proposed liability that governments have undertaken in guaranteeing the payments that the MSEB would be liable under the PPA to the DPC. This concern is applicable with greater force in the case of the GoM. This amounts to a total exposure of well over Rs 2,00,000 crore.

This concern has been expressed on a number of occasions within the government. In a letter dated 24 August 1994, from the Finance Secretary, to the Power Secretary, GoI, the former wrote that the size of "the potential liability for a 1000 MW plant, (was) around Rs 3000 crore per year (around US $ 900 million per year for 1000 MW); around

Rs 12,000 crore per year for the 7 'fast track projects' for over ten years...".[68] The Department of Economic Affairs, MoF wrote that "...the total exposure on the Government of India counter guarantees...around US $ 2.5 billion (annually), for the 7 fast track projects; around Rs 10,000 crore (every year)...".[69] The Department of Economic Affairs had also expressed a fear that the "...risk of the counter guarantees being invoked was not unreal given that SEBs had been defaulting in payments...".[70]

Even an academician like Dr Kirit Parikh, in a letter to the Prime Minister had expressed serious reservations about the Guarantees. He wrote that "The risk of these guarantees being invoked is not too farfetched...".[71] He also warned the Prime Minister that there would a "serious financial crisis" if "all seven fast track projects are given 90 per cent load factor (LF) guarantee and a price of 7 US cents per unit".[72]

The Central Government's Initial Stance

The Government of India had decided on 10 October 1992, not to extend any guarantees at all to the project. In a meeting of the FIPB, the record clearly indicates that Enron had requested the government of India to guarantee the MSEB's obligations.

The government replied that

Mr Verma firmly rejected the proposal and stated that the

---

[68]Letter dated 24 August 1994 from the Finance Secretary, GoI to Power Secretary, GoI.

[69]Letter dated 19 April 1994 from the Department of Economic Affairs, MoF, GoI to the MoP, GoI.

[70]*Ibid.*

[71]*Ibid.*

[72]Letter dated 23 September 1994 from Dr. Kirit Parikh (Member, renegotiating team of GoM in November 1995) to the PM, GoI.

Government of India's guarantee in such a case is not possible. If the Government of Maharashtra guarantees the payments of the MSEB, the question of the Central Government giving further guarantee would raise issues of a constitutional nature.[73]

Two decisions were taken at that meeting: that the return on equity for Enron in the project would be in rupees, and that no government guarantee could be given.

Of course both these decisions were reversed. There is nothing on record indicating their reasons for doing so.

The Government of India's Guarantees

The Republic of India has staked all its assets (including those abroad, save diplomatic and military) as surety for the payments due to the DPC by the MSEB. The total minimum exposure of the GoI is to the tune of at least Rs 35,000 crore, US $ 300 million for in addition to the 695 MW of power. This is an addition of 0.97 per cent to the then existing capacity of 71,000 MW.

Some Relevant Clauses of the GoI's Guarantee

The GoI "waives any right of immunity which it or any of its assets now has or may acquire in the future in any jurisdiction". The GoI, further, "consents generally in respect of the enforcement of any judgment or award against it in any such proceedings to the giving of any relief or the issue of any process in any jurisdiction in connection with such proceedings (including, without limitation, the making, enforcement or execution against or in respect of any assets whatsoever irrespective of their use or intended use of any order or judgment that may be made or given in connection

---

[73]Minutes of the FIPB meeting dated 10 October 1992.

therewith)"; …"assets shall be taken as excluding present or future premises of the mission…and…military property or military assets…".

The State Guarantee

On 10 February 1994, a Guarantee was signed by the Government of Maharashtra to irrevocably and unconditionally guarantee to pay to the DPC any and every sum of money which the MSEB owes the DPC under the PPA.

The total contingent liabilities amount to a total of about 35 billion dollars, i.e., about Rs 1,10,000 crore at the exchange rate of Rs 36 to the dollar. In the event that the rupee to dollar depreciation continues at the rate it has been doing for the last fifty years and in the event of oil prices continuing to increase at the rate they have been for the last thirty years, the total contingent liabilities would amount to between 2,00,000 crore rupees and as much as 3,00,000 crore rupees.

Some Relevant Clauses of the State Guarantee

Guarantee of the MSEB payment Obligations: The Guarantor hereby irrevocably and unconditionally Guarantees to the Company (as a secondary obligor) to pay to the Company, within 7 calendar days following submission by the company of a demand in accordance with Clause 1(B), any and every sum of money which the MSEB is liable to pay to the Company under or pursuant to the PPA and shall fail to pay in accordance with the terms of the PPA.

Indemnity: The guarantor undertakes, as primary obligor, to indemnify and keep indemnified the company against any loss sustained or incurred by the Company by reason of the invalidity, illegality or unenforceability of any of this Guarantee or the provisions of this Guarantee or the PPA and the amount of such loss shall be the amount which, but for such invalidity, illegality or unenforceability, the company would otherwise have been entitled to recover hereunder or thereunder.

Governing Law: The rights and obligations of the parties under or pursuant to this Guarantee shall be governed by and construed according to English Law.

Sovereign Immunity: The Guarantor unconditionally and irrevocably: agrees that the execution, delivery and performance by it of this Guarantee constitute private and commercial act rather than public or governmental acts; agrees that, should any proceedings be brought against it or its assets in any jurisdiction in relation to this Guarantee or any transaction contemplated by this Guarantee, no immunity from such proceedings shall, to the extent that it would otherwise be entitled to do so under the laws of India, be claimed by or on behalf of itself or with respect to assets... waives any right of immunity which it or any of its assets now has or may acquire in the future in any jurisdiction.

The guarantee promises that the state government will be liable for all of the MSEB's dues to the DPC under the PPA. The state government, for reasons best known to itself, has promised to be obligated even in the event that the PPA and other ancillary agreements were found to be illegal or unenforceable. The agreement and its interpretation would be under the provisions of English law. The government has waived its sovereign immunity as well as claims on all assets that may be covered if an action was brought under the provisions of the guarantee.

The Tripartite Agreement

On 16 September 1994, a Tripartite agreement was signed between the GoI, the GoM, and the Reserve Bank of India. This agreement guaranteed payments to the DPC to the tune of Rs 1500 crore a year by the GoI, in the event that GoM defaulted in its obligations. The RBI is to deduct any such amounts from the state's share of central revenues. The State's RBI account is constitutionally sanctioned and sacrosanct wherein Maharashtra's share of central revenues is deposited. The limit of the guarantee (Rs 1,500 crores) is indexed to the rate of inflation, but rising at a minimum rate of 7 per cent a year.

It is interesting to note that in August 1994, the Finance Department of the GoM made the following observation:

> It is true that, as stated in the agreement, as per the guarantee of the Central Government, whatever amount will be given by the Central Government to the company (DPC) will be directly deducted from the Reserve Bank account of the State Government. As regards this it can be only said that we will have to give up the rights conferred on us by the Indian Constitution.

This observation of the Finance Department was not incorporated in the note being prepared for the Cabinet about the Tripartite Agreement.

Constitutional Issues

The guarantees, their nature and specificity raise a number of questions. The primary question is whether such guarantees could have been given in the first place.

The extent of executive power to issue guarantees is limited by Articles 292 and 293 of the Constitution of India. Article 292 limits the powers to give guarantees to limits fixed by legislature, and limits the total exposure to the amount of the consolidated fund. A similar limitation is placed upon the state by Article 293 which limits the power of the state in guaranteeing loans raised by the state.

It is clear that any state government can at best, subject to the caveat, guarantee loans, i.e., quite explicitly, there is no Constitutional provision for guaranteeing revenues to a third party, much less revenues due to a third party that has contracted with a state corporation. The state government makes the GoM responsible for all payments due to the DPC by the MSEB. These payments to the DPC arise from a contractual obligation of the MSEB to pay the DPC for the supply of power.

On the face of it, it seems that these guarantees are problematic and in almost all probability *ultra vires* and illegal. This position was known to the government, but for reasons that are not clear, the government provided the DPC with a set of guarantees that are unprecedented, not only in this country, but in the commercial history of the world for the last five hundred years.

The Court's Opinion on the Matter

These issues have not been examined by any court. The only ruling on this matter is in the Ramdas Nayak Case which is dealt with in the next chapter. However, it seems that the court equated the guarantees to sovereign guarantees for loans. "The GoI gives sovereign guarantees for loans taken by financial institutions and public sector undertakings, e.g. for purchase of a plane by Air India and Indian Airlines,"[74] and therefrom went on to find that there was no problems with the guarantees.

The specific question of the constitutional validity of the guarantees had not been addressed. Subsequently, two petitions that specifically raised the question of the constitutional validity of the guarantees were dismissed on the basis of the judgement passed in the Ramdas Nayak case.

A petition was filed before the Delhi High Court on various issues of the power policy.[75] In this petition, the Delhi High Court found that the question of "giving of counter guarantees

---

[74]Judgement in WP 1702 of 1994 before the Bombay High Court (The Ramdas Nayak Case).

[75]WP 4362 of 1994 in the Delhi High Court; Sidhraj Daddha and others versus the Union of India and others.

by the Union of India", was "outside the purview of Article 293 of the Constitution", and was "not squarely discussed in the judgement by the Bombay High Court" (referring to the Ramdas Nayak Judgement). The Delhi High Court felt that the Bombay High Court had not addressed the question of the constitutional validity of the guarantees.

However, the Delhi High Court chose not to address the question of guarantees specifically, as it found that the petition appeared to have been filed on behalf of someone. It found that the petitioners appeared to be "acting at the behest" of a particular respondent. The petition was dismissed at the admission stage.

Thereafter there has been no examination of this matter, inspite of the Delhi High Court's findings. No court has examined the question of the constitutional validity of these guarantees so far.

Other Issues

Notwithstanding the question of the constitutional guarantees in the first place, there are specific clauses in the guarantees which are problematic.

Consider that the state guarantee (this is also true of the arbitration agreement) is governed by and is to be interpreted under English law. All contracting parties are Indian (the DPC is a company with unlimited liability registered under the Indian Companies Act, i.e., under the ambit of Indian law) and the cause of action arises in India.

Indian law has been specifically excluded. An issue or question of choice of forum (London in this case) and of law (English law) can only arise where the parties to a contract belong to different jurisdictions. Further, any such choice must be bona fide and honest. But the choice of forum, as well as the choice of law applicable to the agreements effectively eliminates the jurisdiction of any court in India.

Furthermore, the State has waived its sovereign immunity as well as its right of immunity on all its present and future assets i.e. the state government has put an effective lien on all its assets: past, present and future in this respect.

The GoM has also agreed to indemnify the DPC against any loss by the company "by reason of the invalidity, illegality or unenforceability of the Guarantee of its provisions or the PPA". What this means is that even if the guarantee or the PPA or any provision of the PPA is found not to be in accordance with Constitutional provisions or in breach of law, the GoM would still be liable to pay the DPC for all and any losses that the DPC might claim.

12

Public Questioning

National Opposition

Opposition to the project started soon after some details of the proposed agreement became known. The first salvo come from an informal group of high ranking former employees of the government comprising former chairmen of the CEA, some state electricity boards and some members of the National Working Group of the Power Sector that included M.K. Sambamurthi, A.N. Singh, J.K. Bhasin, (all former Chairmen of the CEA); N.S. Vasant, B.N. Ojha, both former Chairmen of SEBs; Hiten Bhaya and Arun Ghosh (former Members of the Planning Commission); S.P. Shukla (former Finance Secretary), Government of India. Their critique focused on the extremely high capital cost, the option of choosing LNG, an imported fuel and the economics of the whole scheme. They were particularly concerned about the impact such projects would have on the finances of the state electricity boards. Their other concern was the impact such a project would have on national industry and BHEL.

The government's reaction to this reasoned critique by a group whose credentials were impeccable was to simply dismiss their concerns as being unreasonable and against national interest. Reacting to this critique, the ministry of power said that "...this (opposition to the policy) will play havoc with the power supply situation in the country creating a shortage at the end of 31.3.1997 nearly double the present shortage."

Some politicians followed suit and a motley group spanning the spectrum from saffron to red and green was in the forefront of the opposition to the project. The first public attack on the project was in Maharashtra when it became a political tool in the hands of the BJP against the then Congress chief minister, Sharad Pawar. The BJP accused him of corruption and said that the project was against national interest and the interests of the state of Maharashtra. The opposition of the BJP was cloaked in a veneer of ideology. The public basis was that of 'swadeshi'. The term and concept much abused by the BJP, seemed to carry with it meanings of a return to an ideal past as well as preferential treatment to Indian industry. This attitude is exemplified by the slogan 'computer chips and not potato chips'. The public stance taken by them was that foreign capital in advanced industries would be welcome and not otherwise. Shri Gurumurthy, the former crusader against Reliance, was in the forefront of the party's theoretical and ideological opposition. The politicians included Shri Munde, the then leader of the opposition in the state assembly.

The opposition of the BJP was and in retrospect seems to have been a knee-jerk reaction motivated by political considerations, rather than even a vague semblance of a considered, rational and principled opposition.

This remains one of the supreme tragedies and of course farces of Indian politics.

The First Round of Legal Skirmishes

On 13 July 1994, WP 1702 of 1994, Ramdas Nayak and another versus the Union of India and others was filed. This was the first of the legal salvos against the project. The case was filed by a member of the BJP, the late Ramdas Nayak and the Rambhau Mhalgi Probodhini, a front organisation for the RSS. The challenge was primarily based on the notion that for such a huge project there ought to have been tenders and that the project had been awarded by secret negotiations.

The other issues that were raised in the petition were that there should be no implementation of core sector projects without transparency and fairness: the guarantees given to the project violate Articles 292 and 293 of the Constitution of India; that the project was so unfair that even the World Bank had objected; that the project ought to have been reviewed by experts, and finally that a *certiorari* be issued against the MoU and the PPA. Further, the petitioners brought in the World Bank view on the project and its decision not to fund the project. The payment guarantees and no business risks along with the high PLF would affect the viability of SEBs.

The CEA was not a party in the case, nor was the concurrence/clearance an issue.

In response, the Chairman of the MSEB, Ajit Nimbalkar, claimed that they did not call for tenders because "Enron Power Corporation is one of the world's leading gas and power companies".[76] This, as seen earlier, is belied by Enron's own published data. However, by attempting to show that the MSEB could not call for tenders Ajit Nimbalkar trapped himself in rather astonishing admissions of ignorance and

---

[76]Affidavit submitted by Ajit Nimbalkar, Chairman of MSEB in Writ Petition No. 1702 of 1994 in the Bombay High Court, Ramdas S. Nayak and Another Vs. Union of India and Others, henceforth referred to as WP 1702 of 1994.

incompetence. In his affidavit he stated: "I submit that floating of the competitive tenders in a project like the present one is most inappropriate. Competitive bids require preparatory exploration and work which is considerably costly and time consuming particularly in the case of power plants".[77] He went on to say that "In the present case there was no preparatory exploration of the type for a plant like the one which the Dabhol Power Company is setting up. Again the competitive bid procedure requires expert knowledge and experience for evaluating the competitive bids which at present is still not sufficiently upto the mark. For evaluation of such specialised projects, it is also necessary to have knowledge of risk identification and allocation which is also not sufficiently developed".[78]

One needs to keep in mind, that in this public interest litigation, no evidence of any kind was produced nor were any documents were examined by the Court. The Court did not examine any specific aspect of the project, no papers on the decision making process of the government were called for. Nor, critically enough, the specificities of the law's requirements examined at all. The petitioners were allowed to examine the 400-page PPA over a lunch break. The fact that neither the petitioners, nor the GoI could point out any specific problems in this document in an afternoon, is perhaps not very relevant.

The High Court's Ruling

On 19 August 1994, a division Bench comprising their Lordships, Justices Saraf and Dudhat of the Hon'ble High Court at Bombay, gave their decision in the case. The Court found that

---

[77] *Ibid.*
[78] *Ibid.*

Nothing was done secretly. There was total transparency at every stage of the negotiations.[79]

Furthermore, the Court ruled that

"We may also make it clear that the petitioners have not alleged any malafides against the respondents. There is nothing to show that anybody was being favoured for any specified reason. The grievance of the petitioners is on the sole ground of the failure to follow the usual procedure of inviting tenders, which as stated by us earlier, is not an invariable rule. In our opinion, in the present case it may not be an appropriate mode. Negotiation was the only appropriate mode which has been done in a most reasonable manner. The decision has been arrived at after long deliberations and discussions and after consideration of all relevant factors...".[80]

The Hon'ble High Court held that, after

Applying above principles to the facts of the case, ... We do not find any impropriety in the Power Purchase Agreement entered into between the MSEB and Respondent No. 8, the Dabhol Power Company. Finalisation of a deal by negotiations, as has happened in the present case cannot, per se, be termed as illegal.[81]

This judgement of the Bombay High Court proved to be a landmark one. Subsequently, there were a string of litigations on various aspects of the Enron matter. However, each and every petition that followed was dismissed at the admission stage itself on the basis of this judgement under the doctrine of *res judicata*. It is necessary to appreciate that this doctrine

---

[79]Judgement of the Hon'ble High Court of Bombay in WP 1702 of 1994.
[80]*Ibid.*
[81]*Ibid.*

of *res judicata* is applicable if and only if the specific matter or issue that was raised or ought to have been raised, has been examined by the courts and a judgement issued on the same. Simply put, the courts would not consider reexamining the matter. For example, two petitions that challenged the constitutional validity of the guarantees were dismissed at the admission stage on the basis of *res judiciata*.[82]

Educating Indians

Extracts from the Testimony of an Enron Employee, Ms

---

[82]*Res judicata*: if one issue (or cause of action) has been heard and decided by a court between two parties then the same parties cannot ask for a retrial in the matter again. Res judicata therefore is between the same parties and on the same cause of action or issue.

Further refinement to this principle is contructive res judicata. This has two implications. First, where persons sue in representative capacities, other persons claiming in that same capacity or through the earlier party cannot sue again. One of the tests of representative actions is the inability of a person to compromise or withdraw a claim (because that would bind others whom he represents). The Ramdas Nayak case was finally withdrawn after the BJP renegotiated the contract. The Ramdas Nayak case was therefore clearly political and not public interest (it was withdrawn when the political/personal interest was satisfied).

Secondly: where a person sues on one cause of action/issue but omits to use any matter or issue which might and ought to have been a ground of attack or defence in the former suit, he cannot reagitate that issue (even if that issue was not heard or decided in the earlier matter).

This rule requires: that the party must have full knowledge of the matter; (Ramdas Nayak of course, had no knowledge of anything: he even failed to challenge/point out the basic breach of the tariff notification under section 43(A) of the (5)A which did not merely stare one in the face but in fact, jumped out and slapped you in the face.)

Ought: there was an obligation on him to agitate that issue as part of the earlier action.

The challenge in Ramdas Nayak's petition was on a ground where concurrence/clearance issued by the CEA could not be a ground of attack or defence: the words attack or defence are used in the section.

Linda Powers in her sworn testimony to the Committee on Appropriations, U.S. House of Representatives, are reproduced below.

"Working through this process (of evolution of Enron's Dabhol project) has given the Indian authorities a real and concrete understanding of the kinds of legal and policy changes needed in India, and has given the Indian banks a real and concrete understanding of sound project lending practices. Moreover, our company spent an enormous amount of its own money—approximately $20 million—on this *education* and project development process alone, *not including any project costs.*" (emphasis supplied)

An appropriate conclusion that can be inferred from the above statement is left to the reader. Attention is simply drawn to the fact that these expenses are in addition to all legitimate project costs.

Additional extracts are reproduced herein below.

"Private parties, like our company and others, are now able to develop, construct, own, and operate private infrastructure projects in these countries. In the process of doing so, private parties are able to achieve the two things which U.S. foreign assistance efforts are long been trying (without much success) to achieve: (1) *the projects are serving as action-forcing events that are getting the host countries to finally implement the legal and policy changes long urged upon them.*" (emphasis supplied)

CIA's Involvement?

An interesting report was filed by Chidanand Rajghatta from Washington titled "CIA Helped Enron Bag State Contract" in the Indian Express dated 22 February 1995. The report was apparently based on a testimony to the US Congress by the Director of the CIA. It appears this testimony was in the context of the usefulness of the CIA for US commercial interests. This is one key document that the author has been unable to procure to date. However, the key extract from the testimony is reproduced below:

> In another case involving Enron and its bid for a power plant in Maharashtra, the Americans won the contract thanks to valuable inputs from the CIA on the competitive strategies of rival bidders.

I suppose it may be of interest to recollect that there were no 'rival bidders' in the first place. Therefore, the mystery remains.

The 26th Report of the Parliamentary Standing Committee on Energy

The Dabhol project and other power projects came under pointed scrutiny from the Parliamentary Standing Committee on Energy. All parties concerned including the Ministry of power, the CEA, the Secretary of Finance as well as the DPC gave false and misleading testimonies before the committee.

For example, the CEA when asked if the tariff of the Dabhol project had been determined before any scrutiny of the project took place, claimed that the tariff was "finalised in December 1994", i.e., well after the CEA scrutinised the project and gave clearance to the project, which certainly was not the case. The tariff had been finalised by the PPA a year before the CEA's deliberately put false date. Additionally, the CEA had not scrutinised the project at all.

The Finance Secretary claimed to have been "consistently stating" that the cost per unit rather than the cost per MW needed to be defined. He went on to state that "we (the MoF)" do "not do that" (look at the cost per unit) since "we do not have any experts". He went on further to state that the scrutiny of the cost per unit of power had to be done by the CEA. The Finance Secretary presumably forgot his role in the FIPB meeting of November 1993 where he had decisively come to a definite conclusion about the reasonableness of the cost of power from the Dabhol project.

The MoP's testimony was misleading at best. To illustrate, while testifying that the capital costs were not unduly inflated by private investors, it took shelter under the provisions of the ESA. It was very well aware that none of these provisions were in fact followed at all, from the publication of the advertisement before the submission of the project to the CEA to the scrutiny of the cost estimates. However, by pointing to these provisions, the ministry contended that there was no inflation of capital costs.

The DPC lied[83] when it informed the subcommittee that the company "neither insisted nor expected any guarantee" on payment obligations. They went on to continue lying by blandly stating that following the announcement of the policy of counter guaranteeing announced by the GoI, the company simply "took advantage" of the policy.

The committee, which consisted of members of all parties, came to certain unanimous conclusions. The Committee concluded by expressing "grave reservations" about the Dabhol project particularly in respect of its "excessive cost" and the "guaranteed offtake of power" implying backing down of existing power generation. The committee called the guarantees "unjustified". It concluded that the "lack of transparency" was "regrettable" as it "precluded public scrutiny".

The committee's recommendations and observations were not implemented, nor were any of the testimonies examined at all.

---

[83]See chapter on guarantees. The DPC had requested that guarantees be given. The initial approach was, in fact, regretted.

13

The Change in Laws and the Other Projects

Enron had requested that the laws be modified so as make them in conformity with its PPA and not the other way around. The agenda for the change in laws was set in September 1993 by the GoM. In a letter[84] to the GoI, the state government set out the following requests to the central government.

- That the "structure of the tariff as prescribed under the structure of these acts was to be in consonance with Enron's tariff structure proposed under the PPA".
- That the "DPC will have no obligations to provide information to any authority or MSEB other than those prescribed in the PPA".
- That the relevant arbitration provisions under the act will not apply to this PPA.
- That there should be a "guarantee against change of legislation" ...in respect of allowing foreign private sector investment/operation of the plant and "suitable

---

[84]Letter dated 10 September 1993 from the Secretary (Energy), GoM to the Special Secretary, Power, GoI.

amendments to the Electricity Act to prevent MSEB from restraining the operations of Enron Power Plant; as per the statutory powers conferred upon it."

The implications of this are grave. For a commercial agreement, the statute was asked to be amended. The GoI instead of asking the company to bring its PPA in conformity with the laws, not only bent over backward but went on to do what Enron suggested. Even with the passage of time, it is humiliating and pathetic, to read this.

Monetary Implications

Officially, the minimum return Enron will secure, on its purported equity, is about US $ 4 billion over the life of the contract. The change of five words in the law allows it an additional 3 billion dollars. Further, the rate of return is computed on admittedly "very-very inflated capital costs" as well as very high rates of interest. Effectively, the rate of return on real equity is limitless.

Parliament had mandated that "a reasonable return on equity" be provided. This was set at the prevailing RBI rate plus an additional 5 per cent in the case of licensees like the Tatas, who also have generating plants. For "generating companies", i.e., entities that simply generated electricity and supplied it to the SEBs who in turn would distribute the electricity, the return on equity was set at 16 per cent on the paid up capital. This is a reasonably generous return because it is added on to the price of electricity and to that extent is guaranteed. It is to be borne in mind that the SEBs are mandated only 3 per cent return on assets by the law, the value of the assets being calculated on a depreciated basis. The effective return on equity to SEBs would translate to about 7–8 per cent on the paid up capital.[85] There were additional incentives built into the framework.

---

[85]Very approximately, debt to equity ratio of 70:30; etc.

In any case, the official return on equity as computed by the CEA for Enron was 25 per cent in the fifth year ranging to 55 per cent in the fifteenth. These are post tax returns. Income tax that the company would pay was a pass through, i.e., MSEB would pay the income taxes. This official rate of return is beyond any acceptable margins at any level.

The official rate of return of 16 per cent would have rendered the PPA illegal. Therefore, as suggested by Enron's lawyers, a series of surreptitious amendments to the laws were issued by bureaucratic fiat, bypassing Parliament's mandate completely.

Shortly after the PPA was signed, there was a notification amending the primary notification. This new notification allowed for the additional rate of return on equity. Officially, in Enron's case the rate of return could now be 31.5 per cent.[86]

On 15 February 1994, the GoM wrote to the GoI that:

> The main issue, of course, is that the tariff proposal in the Dabhol Project deviate from the GoI's tariff notification. It is now necessary for the CEA to issue a suitable amendment under Section 43-A of the Electricity Supply Act. MSEB apprehends that unless such an amendment is issued, the PPA itself may run into legal difficulty.[87]

In response, the GoI amended tariff notification, arrogating to itself the right to approve deviating tariffs.[88]

---

[86]The rate has been set on the mere availability of the power station. By simply making the station in a position to be able to deliver power, the powers that be allow for a rate of return, that is the highest in the world. The form for the availability for gas based stations internationally is about 98 per cent and above. In India it is of the order of 90 per cent and above. A gas turbine by its very nature is available most of the time.

[87]Letter dated 15 February 1994 from the MSEB to the GoI.

[88]Notification issued by the GoI dated 22 of August 1994.

The entry of Enron, on the terms that it received, led to the breakdown of nearly all systems across the board. All sorts of companies, both local and obscure ones from the USA in particular, jumped into the arena. Across states, anyone, without the slightest capital or expertise, signed MoUs with the states and or the SEBs for the purchase of power.

Nearly every state went berserk. In Andhra Pradesh, the government signed 64 MoUs in a single day. These, if implemented would have involved purchases involving payments of over Rs 5,00,000 crore. There is no parallel in the last 500 years of commercial history, of lunacy on such an unparalleled scale.

The then power secretary of the state, protested but to no avail. He then resigned in disgust. In this sordid saga, he seems to be one of the few public servants who acted on the dictates of his conscience and in the public veal.

Perhaps an advertisement in the *Business Standard* sometime in early 1998 summarises the situation. The HSEB had apparently signed an MoU with two promoters for hydel plants. These were tiny, but nonetheless involved the purchase involving nearly a 1000 crore rupees. Two years later, the HSEB was trying to track the promoters down. Even the registered addresses of the companies were fake. The HSEB was unable to send a notice to them.

Some projects were put on a "fast track" status by the government for reasons best known by the government. Perhaps a look at the next section which examines some of these 'fast track' projects could convince the reader.

The Cogentrix Project

The brief facts are as follows. The Karnataka State Electricity Board (KSEB) signed a PPA for a 1000 MW coal-fired power plant at Mangalore with an American company, Cogentrix Energy Inc. The coal was to be imported. Like all PPAs, the

KSEB promised to purchase power from the company at an 85 per cent load factor for a period of thirty years. This means that at the price agreed upon, the KSEB would pay Cogentrix about Rs 2000 crore in the first year the plant is operational (these payments were to be indexed to the dollar among other indices). The total contract is valued conservatively at Rs 75,000 crore. The situation for the KSEB is much worse (as compared to the MSEB) since the KSEB has to pay nearly 80 per cent of its total revenues for a 25 per cent increase in capacity.

In view of the decision to invite private sector participation, the Government of Karnataka (GoK), like a lot of state governments, had issued an office order that allowed the State Government to enter into MoUs for this project with foreign companies.[89] This office order had specified that these MOU's were to be signed with companies provided they took projects exclusively (on their own) or in joint sector.[90] The Government had not issued any tenders internationally or nationally inviting interested parties to bid for the project.[91] The State Cabinet issued an office order authorising the State Government to enter into MoUs for 250 MW projects in Mangalore and Bangalore.[92] The capacity of 250 MW was presumably decided after an examination of the current and projected needs in the state.

On 30 July 1992, the GoK signed two MOU's[93] with Cogentrix Energy Inc. in the US for two plants of 500 MW capacity each at Mangalore and Bangalore respectively.

In express violation of its own orders, the GoK in the MoU

---

[89]Government Order No. 108 of the government of Karnataka dated 24.7.92.

[90]*Ibid.*

[91]Affidavit of the Government of Karnataka in Writ Petition No. 10696 of 1997 in the Karnataka High Court. (herein after referred to as WP 10696 of 1997)

[92]*Ibid.*

[93]MOU's between the GoK and Cogentrix Energy Inc. dated 30.7.92.

with Cogentrix Energy Inc., allowed Cogentrix to bring in any partners they wished. Additionally, in another explicit violation of the GoK's orders, the MoUs signed with Cogentrix Energy Inc., were for two 500 MW Projects. The government had only sanctioned two projects of 250 MW capacity. These are non trivial errors. The additional 500 MW capacity would mean payments of Rs 30,000 crore.

If all this was not bad enough, Cogentrix Energy, in 1992 was a small, in fact a very small company. It's total paid up equity was less than Rs 45 lakhs.[94] (it is not a typographical error). Additionally, at that time the debt to equity ratio was 19.2:1.[95] Most Indian or for that matter international companies have debt to equity ratios ranging from 0.5:1 to about a maximum of 4:1. Ratios of this nature are unheard of anywhere in the world and in most cases indicate a basket case. Further, the company had no international experience, had never undertaken any project of more than 250 MW. The total installed capacity of the company was less than 1000 MW. To put these financial figures in some perspective, the equity base of the NTPC is several thousand fold more and its debt equity ratio was 2:1. Tatas or Reliance or even the smallest Indian energy company would be in substantially better financial health. What emerges from this, is that this was a company that could not under any circumstance, be in a position to execute a project, that by its own estimate would cost Rs 4000 crore. Even the mandatory equity contribution would be at least Rs 1000 crore. Cogentrix would absolutely not be in a position to contribute even a fraction of this sum from its own pockets.

Like Enron the saga ought to have ended there. However, it continued...

On 19 November 1992, a new government assumed office

---

[94]Annual Report of Cogentrix energy as quoted in WP 10696 of 1997.
[95]*Ibid.*

in Karnataka and decided to re-examine all the MoUs. Their apparent motive was to make sure that the selection of parties for the power projects was through "adequate publicity", to ensure "fair play" and "protect the good name of the administration".[96] These motives were given short shrift by specific officers of the central government who were concerned that a review would "adversely affect foreign investments".[97] A committee of secretaries of the state government therefore recommended the approval of the project on 27 February 1993.[98]

On 18 March 1993, a Government Order permitted Cogentrix to sell power directly to industrial units at mutually negotiated rates.[99] This would have been fair enough, but as usual for reasons that are not clear, this order was overturned and thereafter the government asked the KSEB to buy all the power from Cogentrix. This single decision involves guaranteed payments of over Rs 2000 crore a year for a period of thirty years, i.e., a guaranteed purchase order of Rs 75,000 crore to a company whose total equity was Rs 45 lakh.

Thereafter, again for reasons that are not clear the plant at Bangalore was 'cancelled' and the plant at Mangalore was allowed to be doubled, i.e., a capacity of 1000 MW was allowed for the Mangalore plant. Notwithstanding the inadequacy of an examination of such a broad parameter as the physical location of the plant, it now appears that the project was 'allowed' to be shifted to Cogentrix's claim that financing such a plant would be easier.[100] With this shift of location a new set of problems emerged for the state

---

[96] Additional Statement of the GoK in WP 10696 of 1997.
[97] *Ibid.*
[98] *Ibid.*
[99] *Ibid.*
[100] *Ibid.*

government. By the government's own admission, all of this power was not required in Mangalore and would need to be evacuated to Bangalore. This evacuation of electricity from Mangalore to Bangalore required new transmission lines connecting the two places. The transmission lines required an additional investment of Rs 750 crore to bring the power to Bangalore. Additionally, the Electricity Board would incur transmission and distribution losses to the extent of upto 20 per cent for the evacuation of this power to Bangalore where it was required.

Despite the problems the project continued. The state government was to sign a PPA with Cogentrix. In January 1994, the central government made it a pre-condition to have the PPA vetted by independent experts for issue of sovereign guarantee for the obligations of the state electricity board. A leading team of experts from India (TERI—Tata Energy Research Institute), together with American and German firms of international repute issued a report that was severely critical of the PPA. They commented that the PPA was one sided, that the capital cost of the plant was too high, along with a host of other observations. Consider just one single observation. The report after examining the technical aspects of the project concluded that the heat rate of the generating units was too high compared to that of international plants with equivalent capacity.

What the technical jargon boils down to is that on this single item Cogentrix was either getting in secondhand and hopelessly outdated equipment, or that if it were using state of the art equipment, it stood to gain about Rs 70 crore a year as hidden profits on this single count. Additionally, the padding in the capital cost and other such factors would add very substantially to the company's profits at the expense of the exchequer.

This report is to date 'secret' and has simply been ignored by the government.

On 30 August, 1994 a PPA was signed by the KSEB with the Mangalore Power Corporation (MPC). Cogentrix was the sole promoter of this company. General Electric Capital was claimed by Cogentrix to be a partner in the project. However, General Electric Capital did not hold a single share in MPC.

After the PPA was signed in January 1995, the MPC submitted a "techno-economic feasibility report". Furthermore, the MPC described itself as a "subsidiary of General Electric Capital" inspite of the latter not holding a single share in MPC. Thereafter, in July 1995, General Electric Capital officially dissociated itself from the project for reasons that are not public.

In August 1995, a company from Hong Kong, Chinalight and Power was brought in as a "co-sponsor" in the project. The MoU entered into between the two parties has not been disclosed. The balance sheet of the MPC for a fifteen-month period submitted to the Registrar of companies, Bangalore, in August 1995, did not show any expenses incurred in India or abroad. This continues through September 1996. The balance sheet of the MPC for the year that ended March 1996, does not account for the amount spent by the sponsors abroad. However, between 1992–1996, the balance sheet of Cogentrix shows approximately Rs 175 crore incurred as "developmental expenses". Additionally, the sum of about HK$ 112 million and HK$ 68 million was written off from the balance sheet of Chinalight and Power, a part of which presumably was for "developmental expenses" of the Indian project.

Finally, in response to Writ Petition No. 10696 of 1997 in the Karnataka High Court, filed by Mr Arun Agrawal that brought these facts to light, on 27 February 1998, a division Bench of the High Court of Karnataka, led by the Hon'ble Chief Justice Sethi in its judgement issued a directive for a CBI inquiry into the matter under its supervision. The order stated that the inquiry would be finished in a year. However, this order of the Karnataka High Court was stayed without assigning any reason by a Supreme Court Bench led by the Hon'ble Chief Justice Punchi. The matter is pending to date (October 1999).

The Bhadrawati Project

The Mittal project ('Bhadrawati Project') is a coal based project. The project includes captive coal mines located near the project. The size of the plant is 1082 MW. At current exchange rates, the capital cost is estimated to be Rs 5.27 crore per MW. About 75 per cent of the cost of the project is indexed to a basket of currencies including the French franc, the British pound and the American dollar. In all likelihood, the capital cost of the project may rise to as much as Rs 6 to 7 crore per MW on account of currency depreciation. The major share holders are Ispat industries, GEC Alsthom and EdF of France with the Mittals retaining a majority holding. The MSEB holds the rights to buy upto 30 per cent of the equity at financial closure.

The plant is expected to run on coal from captive mines for which a separate holding company has been set up. The two captive mines, at Baranj and Lohara villages, very near a huge ordinance complex, have reserves estimated at a minimum of 114 million tonnes. The cost of developing these mines is US$ 350 million (about Rs 1,400 crore currently) as per the PPA. The base price of coal has been set at Rs 745 a tonne. This base price has been expressed as prices as of January 1, 1995, with provisions for escalation built in. Interestingly enough the base price of coal in 1997 terms from new mines in the same area has been estimated by TERI to be between Rs 528 to Rs 650 a tonne i.e. a mark up of at least 15 per cent to as much as 43 per cent on the price of coal.

Large parts of the PPA for this project appear to have been

copied almost verbatim from the Enron PPA. Specific provisions include major arbitration in Thailand or Singapore under the provisions of the laws of the Netherlands.

Exemptions identical to those received by Enron have been incorporated. These include a complete reinterpretation of electricity laws, exemption from Section 10(15)(iv) and Section 10(6A) of the Income Tax Act 1961, from Section 205A(3) of the Companies Act, from the Bombay and Maharashtra Sales Tax Act, from payment of stamp duty and payments of water tax and octroi.

At current exchange rates, the minimum payments by the MSEB in the first year amount to Rs 2198 crore. By the time the project goes on-line, these may be about 20–30 per cent higher. This contract is valued at a minimum of Rs 50,000 crore. The NPV of the contract is of the order of Rs 30,000 crore.

The Patalganga Project

This project is to be set up by Reliance Industries in Maharashtra. I am not going into the details of this project, including correspondence of the company with the CEA here. Perhaps a single item from the Report of the Comptroller and Auditor General of India,[101] released in April 1998, would suffice.

The PPA was entered into in August 1996 for setting up a gas based plant with capacity of 410 MW at Patalganga. The location of the plant was changed from Nagothane to Patalganga after award of project. Reduced completion period of 24 months against 36 months initially was one of the reasons accorded for change in location. However, corresponding reduction in interest during construction

---

[101]The Report of the Comptroller and Auditor General of India for the year ended 31 March 1997, released in April 1998.

(forming part of project cost) was not given resulting in undue benefit of Rs 20.90 crore *per annum* (emphasis in original) to RPPPL in form of higher capacity charges.

The saga continued in other states. The interested reader is referred to the 26th Report of the Standing Committee on Energy for details of the transfer of the Zero Unit Project of Neyveli Lignite Corporation to an NRI Shri Sharad Tak overnight. The situation is much the same in Goa, Haryana, Andhra Pradesh, and many other states.

14

The "Cancellation" of the Project

The project generated much controversy in Maharashtra. Of the two main opposition parties (the BJP and Shiv Sena), the BJP was in the forefront of the opposition to the project on a number of grounds. Their primary contention was allegations of malfeasance or corruption at the highest level. Their opposition to the project was from the very inception of the project. The BJP and the RSS had in July 1994 started legal proceedings against the company and the government (see the chapter on legal proceedings for more details). These were unsuccessful. Gopinath Munde, leader of the BJP and the leader of the opposition in the legislature, led the opposition within the BJP. In the debate in the legislative council, he had alleged that there had been massive profits to the then CM, Shri Pawar.

The elections to the state assembly were announced in January 1994. The Sena and the BJP alliance platform in the elections was based on two main grounds—allegations of corruption against the then Chief Minister Sharad Pawar in the Enron project and his alleged links with the underworld.

The Enron platform was made to be a key issue in the elections. Munde with a few other leaders from the BJP visited the Enron site and promised to throw "the project in the Arabian Sea". He went on to add that "I have come here to promise you that I am not going to remain in the background of this fight against Enron but would be fighting along with you till the time Enron is removed from this land".[102] Allegations of payoffs were made at every public meeting in the state.

The Leakage of the PPA

The matter heated up in the media when the *Business Line* newspaper of 21 March and the *Frontline* issue of the 7 April, both of The Hindu Group, carried long and detailed articles on the PPA which had been kept secret up till then. The articles examined some aspects agreement of the deal.[103]

Unilateral Waiver of the Conditions Precedent

The BJP and the SS alliance won the elections in February 1995. They took office two months later. In the interim period of two months before the alliance actually took over the reins of power, the caretaker government of Sharad Pawar waived the conditions precedent in the PPA. Enron had sent a letter to the MSEB on seeking waiver of the conditions precedent to the PPA. The chairman of the MSEB noted "received" on the letter. A subsequent identical copy of the letter in the government files now has the noting "accepted".

In any case, the purported 'unilateral waiver of the

---

[102]Taped speech of Shri Munde, copy available with Mangesh Chavan through the author.

[103]Ram, N. and Sridhar, V., "The Dabhol Deal", *Business Line*, 21 March 1995; Sridhar, V., Ram, N. and Perez, C., "The Scandalous Enron Deal", *Frontline*, 7 April 1995.

conditions precedent' now made the PPA a contractually binding and enforceable document. Until then, the PPA was not contractually binding. This proved to be extremely useful to Enron a few months later.

In conformance with their manifestos, the new ruling alliance of the BJP-SS immediately began investigation into the award of the contract, the economics of the project and the consequences for Maharashtra if the project were to go ahead.

The Maharashtra government transferred Ajit Nimbalkar, chairman of the MSEB, almost immediately. It went on to form a high level official committee to investigate the deal.

On 3 May 1995, a Cabinet sub-committee[104] was constituted by the GoM, to review the Enron project and to report whether the project "subserves the interest" of the state. The committee was headed by the deputy chief minister and several other ministers including the ministers for revenue, finance, industry and law were its members. The committee's terms of reference included going into the reasons for not inviting competitive bids, whether there was any secrecy in relation to the discussions and negotiations, whether the capital cost of the project was reasonable, whether undue favours and concessions were given, whether the rates for power from the Dabhol plant were reasonable, and others.

The deliberations went on for two months. The committee held public hearings[105] in the matter in which both proponents, opponents and Enron itself were given an opportunity to make detailed presentations on the various issues within the committee's purview.

The committee had complete access to all the files[106]

---

[104]The Secret report of the Cabinet subcommittee to review the Dabhol Power project. ("the Cabinet Sub-Committee Report").
[105]The Cabinet Sub-Committee Report.
[106]*Ibid.*

available with the Maharashtra government. They also had access to all files maintained on the project by the department of energy and many other documents related to the deal.[107] After two months of examination and detailed deliberations, the official Cabinet sub-committee reported to the cabinet of Maharashtra at the end of July, 1995.

The report is a damning and a reasoned indictment of the project. It begins by recounting in detail the circumstances under which the deal was signed. The World Bank reports on the deal are referred to in detail. The report observes that the negotiations were conducted with the "sole objective" of seeing that Enron was "not displeased".[108] It then goes on to answer in great detail all the arguments raised by the project proponents.

The first conclusion[109] reached by the committee was that the previous government had "committed a grave impropriety". This was because the previous government had resorted to "private negotiations on a one to one basis with Enron" under "circumstances which made the Enron/MSEB arrangement on Dabhol lack transparency". It went on to conclude that there were absolutely "no compelling reasons not to involve a second contender for Dabhol". It strongly disapproved of "this one to one negotiations with Enron" that violated "standard and well-tested norms of propriety for public organisations".

On the question of "whether undue favours and concessions"[110] had been granted to the project, the committee came to the "irresistible conclusion" that "several unseen factors and forces seem to have worked to get Enron what it wanted". It went on to conclude that "several unusual features of the negotiations and final agreement" in the report

---

[107] *Ibid.*
[108] *Ibid.*
[109] *Ibid.*
[110] *Ibid.*

make it clear that whatever Enron wanted was granted without demur.

The committee's conclusion on the question of capital costs and the rates for power from the Dabhol plant was that the "capital cost of DPC project was inflated".

It went on to say that "because of the denomination of tariff for power in US dollars and other reasons", the consumer would "have to pay a much higher price for power than is justified". This was in its view "clearly not reasonable".

Further "such high cost power as Enron envisages" would "in the immediate future and in the long run adversely affect Maharashtra and the rapid industrialisation of the state and its competitiveness".

Finally, the committee took the view that the "real environmental issue" was "whether such a huge power project should be located in such an unpolluted part of Maharashtra and whether there is any other part of the state where it could have been located..."

The sub-committee after having examined these issues and having "listed the deficiencies", unanimously recommended that "the arrangement in force" was "not tenable" because of the "infirmities pointed out" in the "terms and conditions" of the contract. It therefore, recommended that Phase II of the project be cancelled and Phase I repudiated.

Based on the cabinet sub-committee's recommendations the cabinet of Maharashtra unanimously decided to cancel the contract. Two days later, on 3 August 1995, the Chief Minister of Maharashtra made a formal announcement on the floor of the House. In his speech he stated that the GoM had decided "to scrap phase 1 and cancel phase 2 of the project". In a speech in Marathi, laced with racy metaphors, the CM made a number of observations. Parts of the official translation of the Marathi speech, which do not however quite capture the flavour or force of the original are given below.

He started his speech by recounting the circumstances and

the haste with which the deal was signed. "Enron came, they saw and they conquered" is the phrase used by the CM to describe the haste with which the MoU was signed within three days. He mentioned that despite the World Bank's and the CEA's view on the MoU as being a "one sided" process, all "important activities were completed within 30 days". "The horoscope of the project was cast on that day itself and this sowed the seeds for future problems. The previous government by "one to one discussion with Enron" had "done an uneconomic financial deal which the state cannot afford".

Referring to the absence of tenders in this project, he said that in the case of "such big projects", it was a "general practice to give the opportunity to tender". However, in this case, no "satisfactory explanation was brought" before the CM as to "why this opportunity was not given to any other foreign investor" and that the "idea has not stuck to anybody". Enron had "hypnotised in such a way" that the "state government had not seen the shortcomings of this agreement. If three to four investors had been asked to give their proposals for the project, there would have been competition amongst them and thus it would have been in the interest of the State if the agreement had not become ex-parte".

The CM stated, he was "aware" that the Court had given a "verdict that no unfair practice had taken place by not inviting competitive tenders and by keeping the dealings confidential". The court had also ruled that "the practice of not inviting competitive tenders" was "not illegal". However inspite of this ruling by the court, since "public money is involved", it was "necessary to invite competitive tenders" to ensure the "transparency of the deal". He went on to say that even the central government, after having realised its error, had now "changed its policy and made it compulsory" to "invite competitive tender(s)". After scrutinising all the documents available with the state government and the

MSEB, the CM said that it was not "possible to conclude on the basis of these documents what totally took place", and that everyone was "deprived of information regarding the terms and conditions of this agreement under the pretext of commercial agreement secrecy".

The CM noted that as "the final tariff depends upon the capital cost", it was "necessary to closely scrutinise the capital cost itself" but it did not "seem to have happened in this case". As the government "did not carry out serious negotiations with Enron," only the "loss" had "come to us". As per the CM's information, this was "the costliest project amongst the similar projects undertaken by Enron in other countries".

While "brooding over a thought", whether the purchase price of power was reasonable or not, he "observed that a wrong impression" was "spread amongst the public that the power purchase rate for this project would be Rs 2.40 per unit only". He went on to disprove it, saying that the price involved was the price at which the MSEB would buy the power, which was "54 per cent of the ultimate cost to consumer". Therefore, it would not "be possible for the consumer to get this power" at a rate less than "Rs 5 per unit". Secondly, even the MSEB would not get the power at the rate of Rs 2.40 per unit because this rate involved the exchange rate of the Indian rupee and the US dollar and the price paid for fuel purchase. The CM felt that "while negotiating the agreement no thought was given to protect the interest of the state and consumers".

He stated that even though the project had been approved by the various departments of the state government, then state cabinet ministry of power and finance, the central government and the Foreign Investment Promotion Board which comprised a high level committee of secretaries of central government, all of them should have "taken more seriously cognizance" of "letters of April and July 93 from World Bank".

The CM concluded by describing the contract as "anti-

Maharashtra", that the contract "smacked of lack of self respect" and was irrational. Accepting the contract in its present form is "like betraying the people of Maharashtra". The "agreement" was "no agreement at all". Therefore, "refusing the agreement even with economic burden is acceptable as it is important to maintain self-respect and interest of Maharashtra". It was also "important to expose the people" who had "entered into such agreement". Therefore, the state government had taken a decision and had asked the MSEB "to initiate necessary legal steps".

Based on the above and the findings of the committee, he announced the state's decision. As the state was "empowered to cancel the second phase of Project" the Cabinet decided "to cancel the same" and had "taken a decision that the Agreement of the first phase" was "to be scrapped". The "work of the Enron project" was "to be stopped" and that "stop work directives" would "be issued".

Enron's Reactions

The cancellation although not totally unexpected, took Enron by surprise. For the next two months the government acted tough, contending that their decision was not open to review. Enron's initial attempts to reach a negotiated settlement were rebuffed, at least publicly. Rebecca Mark, Enron's CEO arrived in Bombay. However, her meeting with Shri Bal Thackeray apparently did not prove to be fruitful.

A team from the DPC then went to New Delhi in the second week of April.[111,112] They met the Union Minister for

---

[111]Joseph Sutton from Enron, Scott Bayman from General Electric, Ashok Mehta vice president of DPC and Sanjay Bhatnagar from Enron Development Corporation.

[112]As reported in the *Economic Times*, 13 April 1995; "State Should Honour Enron Pact: Salve", *Economic Times*, 30 April 1995; "Salve Warns Against Scrapping Enron Project" and the *Indian Express*, 13 April 1995.

Power, N.K.P. Salve, the Finance Minister, Manmohan Singh and others.[113] Manmohan Singh claimed that the project could not be cancelled.[114] Salve asserted that the Centre was determined to go ahead with the project and that the state of Maharashtra should honour the Enron pact, otherwise it would prove very costly not only to the state but also to the country.[115] The delegation also met Pramod Mahajan, general secretary of the BJP. They told him that a review would send the wrong signals to investors. Mahajan's rejoinder was that the American companies had already sent feelers to the Government saying they would be interested in case global tenders were invited for the project.[116]

There was a great deal of pressure from the US government.[117] Their Ambassador, Frank Wisner (who interestingly enough, joined Enron as a Director the day after

---

[113] *Ibid.*

[114] 15. Mundley, Anagha, "Enron Project Cannot Be Scrapped, Says Manmohan Singh", *Times of India*, 7 April 1995.

[115] Anon, "Centre Determined To Go Ahead With Enron Project, says Salve".

[116] 14. Anon, "Advani Shuns Meeting With Enron Team", *Indian Express*, 14 April 1995. Anon, "Advani Refuses To Meet Enron Team", *Times of India*, 14 April 1995.

[117] Sridhar, Krishnaswami, "Enron's Gift to Clinton's Party", The *Hindu*, 26 August 1997.

In another interesting addition to the Democratic Party's fund-raising mess, *Time* reported that four days before the Government in New Delhi gave final approval for the Enron Corporation's $ 3 billion venture in India, the company gave the Democratic National Committee $ 100,000. Enron denied that its "gift" was a repayment for Mr. Bill Clinton's attention.

In "the Scoop" section of the magazine, writer Michael Weisskopf reported from Washington that on November 22, 1995, the U.S. President wrote an "FYI" (for your information) note to the then Chief of Staff, Mr. Thomas "Mack" McLarty and enclosed a newspaper article on the Enron Corporation and the "vicissitudes" of the $ 3 billion power project plant in India.(*contd.*)

finishing his stint in India) made several statements against the cancellation. He also led a seven-member delegation in June to the BJP's leaders in an attempt to pressurize them not to cancel the Enron agreement.[118] The US government itself, through the Energy Secretary, publicly warned India that

> "Failure to honour the agreements between the project partners and the various Indian governments will jeopardize not only the Dabhol project but also most, if not all, of the other private power projects proposed for international financing".[119]

The British Chancellor of the Exchequer, Kenneth Clarke, leading a delegation to India, claimed that "If there is a project that is signed up and the rules are changed, there is bound to be an enormous risk".[120] To this the BJP president, L.K. Advani retorted "We cannot see the reason for his

---

(*contd.*) Mr. McLarty is then said to have contacted the Enron Chairman, Mr. Ken Lay. Over the next nine months Mr. McLarty closely monitored that project with the then U.S. Ambassador in New Delhi, Mr. Frank Wisner; and in the process kept Mr. Lay informed of the administration's efforts.

Mr. McLarty is not in the corridos of power in the White House today and according to the version of *Time*, the Counsellor was even then, "tucked away in the basement". But obviously he had played a crucial role in fund-raising for the Democrats, assisting businessmen who coughed up an estimated $ 1.5 million for the party's coffers. In the case of the Enron Corporation and the India project the White House Special Counsel, Mr. Lanny Davis, had said that Mr. McLarty had acted out of concern for a major U.S. investment overseas.

[118]Ramesh, P.R., "Egged On By MP's Panel, State May Scrap Dabhol Project", *Economic Times*, 2 June 1995.

[119]Anon, "Honour Enron Deal, U.S. Warns India", *Times of India*, 5 June 1995.

[120]Anon, "Enron Decision Key To Fund Flow: Clarke", *Times of India*, 3 June 1995.

excessive interest in an American company's project in India in which the British have no known involvement".[121]

The Pakistan Example

In the last week of July 1996, Pakistan canceled a PPA with Enron for a US $670 million, 782 MW residual oil-fueled power plant, as it found the cost of the project prohibitive. The PPA was for 30 years, according to which the Water and Power Development Authority (WAPDA) of Pakistan had guaranteed to purchase power from Enron.

The Pakistan Government decided to cancel the project despite the fact that Enron was to supply power at a fixed rate of 6.4 cents per KwH. This was lower than the notional Rs 2.40 (or over 6.7 cents) the DPC hoped to charge the MSEB for the power it produced. Also, Enron had assured Pakistan that it would use residual fuels for generating power, not LNG. Unlike India, Islamabad refused to provide a blanket guarantee to Enron. It is evident that despite repeated claims that India had not been overcharged for the DPC power plant, Enron's Pakistani project was far cheaper. The project was to be set up at about US $856,700 per MW of installed capacity. The Dabhol cost worked out to US $920 million for a 695 MW plant in the first phase of the project, around US $1.32 million per MW, thus representing an additional cost of US $463,230 per MW. Maharashtra is paying an extra cost of US $321 million just for the first phase of the project as compared to Enron's Pakistani Project.

Suit Filed by the GoM in the Bombay High Court

Pursuant to the decision of the GoM, the MSEB issued stop work orders to the DPC. The DPC requested clarification

---

[121]Anon, "Don't Pressurize State On Enron, Says Advani", *Times of India*, 7 June 1995.

and thereafter sought arbitration under the state support agreement in London under the provisions of English law.

The state government responded by instituting a suit[122] in the Bombay High Court. The suit sought cancellation of the contract on a number of grounds. The suit was drafted and settled by a panel of leading legal luminaries that included the advocate general of Maharashtra and Mr Fali Nariman.

The government affirmed on oath that, the action on the part of the MSEB in "unilaterally waiving compliance with various Conditions Precedent" was "effectuated and conceived in fraud" and was "not bonafide" and therefore rendered "the agreement as void". It went on to say that the "unholy haste" with which the Financial Closure was "achieved" was "clearly in order to reap the benefit of the huge sum of US$ 20 million" that was spent by Enron, i.e., the government was claiming that the chairman of the MSEB had been bribed by Enron to fraudulently make the PPA binding.

The government stated that the PPA was "null and void ab-initio, inter-alia, on account of its being violative of several statutory provisions, public policy, consumer interest, public interest and interest of the state". Further, the PPA suffered "from the vice of misrepresentation" by Enron and was "conceived in fraud".

It alleged that the PPA was illegal and in total breach of laws. Specifically, the GoM affirmed that the PPA had been "executed in complete contravention of the requirements of Section 29 of the ESA" and that the PPA violated "Section 43A", "Section 18" and "Section 30" of the ESA.

It set up "various acts and conduct" by Enron which were

---

[122]On 6 of September 1995, the GoM instituted Suit No. 3392 of 1995 on the Original Side of the Hon'ble Bombay High Court against DPC and the MSEB.

"deceptive and fraudulent". These included the fact that Enron had misrepresented to the GoM about "the cost of their other power stations" and about the "rate of interest". Further, that Enron had misrepresented information "about the preclosing clearances" and "further fraudulently induced" the MSEB to "agree to a waiver of all these conditions".

The government also stated that the PPA was "contrary to the public policy of this country" as it would "cause a huge loss to the public exchequer on the purchase and sale of power" and "place an unconscionable burden on the electricity consumers of the State".

It submitted to the court that "the provision under the State Support Agreement to be governed by English Law" was not based on "any valid or bonafide ground" and that "opting for the application of English Law by Indian parties in respect of an Indian cause of action is clearly illegal and unconstitutional".

The government took the stand that the "manner in which the transaction was entered into", the "contents" of the "transactions", the manner in which it was "closed" and the manner in which Enron was acting to see that "somehow it is executed" clearly showed that the transaction was "void, illegal, inoperative, incapable of performance, unlawful, contrary to law, public policy and public interest".

The government adduced a compendious volume of documentation from its files to support these contentions, a list of which was annexed to the suit.

The GoM's Submissions to the Arbitration Tribunal

The GoM as a respondent made a similar submission to the arbitration tribunal. It contended that the PPA was never binding and thus its ancillary agreements viz., the State Support agreement and the Guarantee of the GoM were invalid and therefore the arbitration agreements themselves were invalid. Attention is particularly drawn to the explicit allegation of the Maharashtra government that officers and agents of the MSEB were bribed to secure the contracts.

The chairman of MSEB was transferred soon after the present government took office. Absolutely no criminal investigation or for that matter investigation of any kind, was initiated by the GoM despite the very serious allegations.

Extracts are quoted below.

The arbitration contained in the SSA and the GoM Guarantee are governed by Indian law (despite the express choice of English law as the proper law of the SSA and GoM Guarantee) and, by Indian law, those arbitration agreements are invalid…

The circumstances of the present case involve three contracts (of which two are the subject of notice of arbitration) to which an Indian state government are a party and to which the other parties are Indian corporations, statutory and non-statutory;

these contracts were made in India;

the obligations provided for these contracts are also to be performed in India;

there is an allegation of breach of Indian constitutional electoral law and its consequences;

there is an allegation of breach of the public law duties (under Indian law) of an Indian statutory corporation;

there is an allegation of fraudulent inducement of the principal contract and of fraud in connection with its performance, allegations which also impact upon the two ancillary contracts.

…Not only is the making of a bribe a criminal offence. It also means that the officers and agents of the Maharashtra State Electricity Board ("MSEB") who purported to contract on behalf of the board were exceeding their authority. An employee or agent has no authority to bind his principal to a fraudulent transaction. The consequence of this is that the

MSEB were not contractually bound by the actions of their employees or agents purportedly on their behalf. This means that the MSEB never entered into the PPA. It was an agreement made by officers without authority to act. It therefore, does not bind the MSEB. (emphasis added)

"A contract procured by a bribe is illegal and void both under English and under Indian law. The effect of that is to render the PPA illegal and void. Since the SSA and GoM Guarantee are ancillary to and supportive of the PPA, they are also tainted by the same illegality..." (emphasis added)

...the capacity of the officers and agents of the MSEB and their authority to bind the Board in circumstances of bribery and the effect upon the agreements of criminal conduct in connection with the transactions.

15

Enron *Bachao* Desh *Hatao*

The "Revival" of the Project

On 3 November 1995, Ms Rebecca Mark, of Enron, flew down to meet Mr Bal Thackrey, the self-proclaimed hand holding the "remote control", of the Maharashtra government. After Ms Mark met Mr Bal Thackeray, the Government of Maharashtra announced "renegotiations".

The Renegotiation Committee

On 8 November 1995, a renegotiation committee was constituted by the GoM. The committee's mandate itself was interesting. The committee had a mandate to "revive both phases of the project", i.e., these were not "renegotiations" but simply a formality to sanctify a deal that was reached privately. The contract that was canceled was only for the first phase of 695 MW. The committee had been asked to "revive" both phases.

On 19 November 1995, the renegotiation committee concluded these 'renegotiations' and submitted its report.

Farcical is perhaps the only word that can be used in this context. Not only are there absolutely *no* changes in the old contract but matters actually took a turn for the worse.

The government decided to go ahead with the second phase which earlier, was completely optional. It is absolutely critical to appreciate that the "scrapped" agreement, that was so opprobrious, "against the interest of the state" and "contrary to the public policy" was for only the first phase of 695 MW. The earlier contract involved annual payments of U$ 430 million (Rs 1380 crore then) by the MSEB. The MSEB had the freedom, of not taking up the entire project of 2015 MW without incurring any liabilities. The second phase that would use natural gas as a fuel and bring the total capacity upto 2015 MW was completely optional and the MSEB could at any time cancel it or negotiate appropriate conditions or pricing without any penalties.

The 'new' renegotiated contract is the single largest contract in India's history involving total payments to DPC to the tune of US $35 billion.

The observations of the Bombay High Court in its judgment in this matter summarise the sorry situation rather well.

> But once it (GoM) *decided to revive the project, it acted in the very same manner in which its predecessors in office had done. It forgot all about competitive bidding and transparency. The only transparency it claims is the constitution of the negotiating group. The speed with which the negotiating group studied the project, made a proposal for renegotiation which was accepted by DPC, and submitted its report is unprecedented. The negotiating group was constituted by the Government of Maharashtra on 8th November 1995. It was asked to submit its report to the State Government by 7th December 1995. The Committee, we are told, examined the project, collected data on various similar other projects as well as internal bids including data on a similar project executed by Enron in the U.K., held considerable*

negotiations, settled the terms on 15th November 1995, just within a week of its constitution, and submitted its exhaustive report along with data and details to the Government of Maharashtra on 19th November 1995, just 11 days after its formation, much before the 7th December 1995 by which date it was required to submit the same. The speed at which the whole thing was done by the renegotiating group is unprecedented. What would stop someone to say, as was said by the Chief Minister in the context of the original PPA, "Enron revisited, Enron saw and Enron conquered—much more than what it did earlier".

Highlights of the "Renegotiations"

Some of the highlights from the report of the committee are as follows. The capacity was increased by "renegotiations" to a binding 2184 MW. After the "renegotiations", there was absolutely no decrease in tariff. The committee and the GoM simply lied in claiming a lowered Phase 1 tariff, when in fact there was none. The entire project of 2184 MW now involved payments of at least US $ 1400 million (Rs 5,500 crore @ $ = Rs 39) a year for 20 years. The committee claimed to have achieved "significant" reduction in tariff and several "concessions" from the DPC. As events and correspondence revealed, every one of the claims was simply a lie, or a deliberate misrepresentation and fraudulent with an intention to deceive.

Some of the Committee's Contentions

The committee claimed that the "Total project tariff (2450 MW) levellized (sic) tariff" was reduced to "Rs 1.89/kWh (1995) with no capital recovery escalation". Rs 1.89 looks substantially lower than (presumably) Rs 2.40.

It is, however, to be noted that the tariff for Phase 2 had not even been negotiated, therefore there is no question of comparison in the first place. Further, the DPC had written to the CEA on 10 November 1993 that the concept of a levelised rate was not valid in the tariff structure negotiated between the DPC and the MSEB.

The claim that the tariff had been reduced to "Rs 1.89" from "Rs 2.40" is deliberately dishonest.

(i) The earlier tariff of Rs 2.40 (which, too was false) was based on 1997 prices, while the present tariff figure given out is based on 1995 prices, and that too in dollar terms.

(ii) Further, the assumed price of naphtha was arbitrarily low, having no connection to reality. International as well as Indian prices were thirty to fifty per cent higher than the committee's assumptions at the time the committee submitted its report.

(iii) This was later borne out by the DPC's own letter to the CEA. On 7 March 1996, the DPC wrote to the CEA detailing "minor" changes in the project. They wrote that "there is no change in the capacity charges for Phase 1".

The committee made a number of outright assumptions that should not have been made by anyone with commonsense or the slightest knowledge of economics. The assumptions made by Government/RC are deliberately depressed and ignore reality leading to a misleading and extremely low tariff. In fact, both the tariff, and the assumptions used to arrive at the tariff, appear designed to mislead.

While claiming that the starting tariff was Rs 2.22 the committee made the following assumptions:

(i) The value of the rupee to be 32 to $ 1 (While the committee was "renegotiating", the value of the rupee was 35 to $ 1).

(ii) After calculating all payments, based on the assumption that the rupee was valued at 32 to $ 1, they went on to further assume that there would be absolutely no change in the value of the rupee against the dollar for the next 20 years, while providing for payments to be indicated to the dollar.

(iii) There would be absolutely no inflation in the USA for the next 20 years, while providing for tariff to increase with the rate of US inflation.

(iv) The price of LNG would be a constant US $ 3.46/MMBTU (all inclusive). Enron's price as stated to the GoI and the CEA was substantially higher, US $ 4.46 to US $ 5.50/MMBTU.

(v) The regassification price would be in constant rupee terms at Rs 0.17/kWh while the actual payments are in dollars.

(vi) Lastly, it took all the above prices in 1995 prices in $ terms (against 1997 prices in $ terms in the original PPA). This alone bring the prices down by 7 per cent.

The "per MW cost reduced to Rs 2.63 crore from 4.06 crore" was achieved inter alia, the "Reduction of 1580 crore by delinking regassification plant from power plant".

(i) This would presumably reflect in an substantially reduced tariff. On or around June, 1996, the DPC states that it will include regassification in the main plant. There was no change in tariff after adding Rs 1580 crore to the project costs for the regassification plant.

(ii) They claimed that output was increased by dishonestly attributing it to a "change in turbines" from frame 9F to 9FA. Actually 9FA was always approved. The PPA dated 8.12.93 has an entire section devoted to the 9FA turbines.

(iii) They then went on to misrepresent the capacity as 2450 MW, i.e., simply expressed in ISO terms. Until then the capacity was and has the case for the "old project", in every other project in India or for that matter and every where in the world, had been expressed as Net Exportable capacity. This simple disingenuousness, increases the denominator from 2184 to 2450, thereby "reducing costs/MW" by 12 per cent!

While taking credit for the plant to be "converted into multifuel facility" which would allow it to "run on naphtha" at a cost of US $35 million, the committee conveniently omitted to mention that it had always been designed as a multifuel facility that could use naphtha or distillate, whichever was cheaper. In a letter to the MSEB dated 7 December 1994, the DPC wrote that they

"fully expect to explore the naphtha market after financial close. If naphtha is available and can be obtained at lesser price than distillate, DPC will use Naphtha as the situation exists. They have designed the plant and plant equipment to accommodate either fuel".

The committee had been specially directed to look at environmental issues, which as per the government's admission had received inadequate consideration. The renegotiation committee apparently relied on two arbitrary individuals (Dr Chiplunkar and Mr Rotkar) who had very little expertise in the relevant issues as evidenced by their resumes attached to the committee's report.

The committee managed, presumably after intense negotiations, to insist on "substantial environmental safeguards agreed to including local community aspects by imposing 'conditions' upon DPC".

As usual, the conditions that the committee claimed to have imposed, had already been imposed. For example, the committee claimed "to have imposed a term that DPC would plant 150 hectares". However, even in this matter, the committee was pre-empted by the Ministry of Environment and Forests which had imposed a condition, on 5 August 1993, that 1,00,000 trees would be planted in a green belt.

Similarly, the "local community issues" the committee claims to have addressed such as the "construction of hospital, schools" had already been imposed by the Bombay High Court, in August 1994.

These conclusions were presented to the Bombay High Court in April 1996 (see the following chapter), and substantiated by The Report of the Comptroller and Auditor General of India.[123] This report was released in April 1998. The key conclusions reached by the Auditor General of India are reproduced below.

- The PPA was amended in July 1996 after renegotiations for enhanced capacity of 2184 MW with firm commitment for Phase 2 even though the MSEB had an option in the original PPA to cancel Phase 2 at its discretion without any liability.

- The suspension of the project and renegotiation of the PPA merely served to bring down the levelised capacity charges for Phase 2 from Rs 1.58 per kwH to 1.34 per kwH by removal of escalation for capital recovery charges which should not have been agreed to in the original PPA itself. The capacity charges of Rs 1.32 per kwH in Phase 1 as per original PPA was not reduced. Even capital recovery escalation was not withdrawn.

- The levelised tariff payable as per amended PPA works out to Rs 3.35 per kwH against the projected levelised tariff of Rs 2.21/kwH considering compound annual growth rate of 3 per cent for fuel, exchange rate of $ 1= Rs 38.65 as on 28 November, 1997, tax adjustable charges and rupee debt service charges.

The first phase of the project started delivering power in

---

[123]The report of the Comptroller and Auditor General of India for the year ended 31 March, 1997, released in April 1998.

May 1999. The very first bill for a whopping Rs 240 crores seems to have shocked the wits out of the MSEB and the state government. At the rates then charged, the cost per unit amounts to Rs 5 and total payments amount to Rs 1650 crore per year. This is for the first phase only.

16

The Final "Clearances"

The Centre's counter-guarantee was void because of GoM's decision to first "cancel" the contract and thereafter "renegotiate" it without any changes at all in the old contract. Furthermore, the GoM had included the entire project as binding upon the MSEB. This voided the counter-guarantee since it had specified that any change to the PPA would render it void.

To jump slightly ahead of the chronology, in May 1996, a minority government headed by the BJP was installed at the centre. This government lasted for precisely 13 days. It resigned before facing a vote of confidence in the Lok Sabha. In an extraordinary and historically unparalleled decision, on its last day in office, while the debate on the no confidence motion was still on in the Lok Sabha, the cabinet met at "lunch" and ratified the counter-guarantee to be given to Enron, ostensibly on the grounds that if it was not done with the utmost urgency, the GoM would be liable to pay Rs 86 lakh a day. However a writ petition on this and other issues had been already admitted by the Bombay High Court. The government could have waited for the court's verdict.

This Rs 86 lakh per day was the amount to be paid to Enron as per GoM. The "old" PPA that the government claimed to have "cancelled" did not specify any such amount. The new contract was signed three months later, i.e., in August 1996. The figure of Rs 86 lakh a day was an arbitrary number, which has no basis whatsoever, since there was no binding contract of any kind existing at that time. Enron and the GoM colluded to make up this number and the collusion was thereafter abetted by the GoI.

An interesting alternative explanation of this number (Rs 86 lakh) is the following. One of Enron's lawyers in an unrelated article, while referring to the Dabhol project, stated that "the provisions for compensation on termination are set out in an attachment to the PPA".[124] i.e., there may have been a secret annexure to the PPA that the government has seen fit not to be shown even to the courts. (The PPA that the Government filed before the High Court in its suit did not allude to this annexure). However even if this were true, the fact still remains that at the relevant time there was no binding contract.

The Last Hurdle

On 6 April 1996, the Centre for Indian Trade Unions (CITU) and this writer filed a public interest writ petition in the Bombay High Court. The respondents were the GoI, the GoM, the MSEB, the CEA and Enron.

The primary issue raised in the petition was that the CEA's granting clearance/concurrence was a breach of statute and therefore was void.[125]

The petition also raised a number of other issues. These included the question of the GoM's conduct and the suit filed

---

[124]Guarantees for Infrastructure Projects by Jonathan Inman, a partner in the Project Finance Group of Linklaters and Paines. This article was posted on commercenetindia.com. The original source is difficult to track.

[125]Writ Petition 2456 of 1996, Centre for Indian Trade Unions and another versus The Union of India and others filed in the Bombay High Court ('WP 2456 of 1996').

by the GoM. The GoM had filed a suit against Enron (DPC). The government had alleged fraud, illegality; misrepresentation etc., and had claimed that the PPA was "null and void". Consequently, the GoM could not ratify or modify the agreement which the GoM itself claimed was void. Additionally, some other questions were raised including whether the government of Maharashtra could negotiate and or contract with parties it had charged with corruption and fraud and whether the plea of the State of Maharashtra that corruption does not vitiate a contract under the Indian Contract Act is correct in law.[126]

The petition also contended that the GoM, the GoI, the CEA and the MSEB were trustees of the public. The GoM's suit filed in the Bombay High Court against the DPC was to the public benefit and was based on public policy and public interest. Therefore, the suit could not be withdrawn by the government in the absence of cogent reasons. Furthermore, while the suit was pending, the GoM could not permit contracts with persons that it had indicted for corruption, fraud and misrepresentation etc. In the event the GoM disowned its own suit, the court was obliged to order proceedings against the state government for subverting the process of justice, abuse of process, contempt and perjury and whether the suit filed by the GoM was capable of being withdrawn and or compromised, since it was based on public policy and public interest, particularly corruption, and whether it was validly withdrawn. Lastly, the petitioners asked the court to look into the various issues raised by the Cabinet sub-committee and the statements made by the Chief Minister in the Assembly, that were the basis of cancellation of the project that had since been fulfilled.

The petitioners also requested the court to direct the GoM to make the proposed "new" "amended" PPA public and to

---

[126]*Ibid.*

make public the actual rate at which electricity would be sold to the public. Lastly, that the MSEB should comply with the observations in the audit note from the office of the Accountant General.

The petition claimed that the project did not have the necessary clearance issued by the CEA as required by law. If in the event, the respondents took the position that a clearance had been issued by the CEA, such a clearance was clearly in violation of Sections 29 and 32 of the ESA. Copies of letters written by the finance secretary and the letter by the ministry of power to the CEA (see Chapter 4) were adduced as evidence. The sworn suit of the GoM was adopted by the petitioners as additional evidence.

The petition was heard by Justice Srikrishna in the third week of April 1996. During the five days of arguments that took place, the counsel for the GoM and the DPC argued that the petition was barred by *res judicata*, or that all issues raised in the petition had been already decided by the courts and that the petition did not raise any fresh ground. Therefore, it deserved to be dismissed at the stage of admission itself. They went on to argue that Justice Srikrishna's single judge Bench had no jurisdiction to hear the petition. The Counsel for the petitioners Shri Sunip Sen argued that there was obviously no question of *res judicata* and that his lordship's Bench had full jurisdiction over the matter under the rules of the Bombay High Court.

The court considered these arguments and on 28 April 1996, the petition was admitted by the High Court. The court admitted it on the ground that there was no prima facie bar of *res judicata*, the issues raised in this case having been neither considered nor answered in the previous judgments. Furthermore, the petitioners' contentions were the very contentions urged in the suit by the state government to avoid the PPA. It left the question of 'whether the novatio (the "new" PPA) required concurrence of the CEA under the Act' open.[127]

In his order dated 26 April, Justice Srikrishna declared that the petition was tenable before a single judge.[128] The same evening the Counsel for the respondents, (DPC, Enron and the GoM) submitted a written memorandum to the Chief Justice of the Bombay High Court in his chambers. The memorandum stated that the delay due to litigation was costing the DPC Rs 86 lakh per day in interest payments alone and that the matter should be referred to a two-judge Division Bench. These points had been argued by the respondents before Justice Srikrishna and been overruled in his judgement.

On 2 May 1996, an Office Order was issued by the High Court "pursuant to the directions given by the Hon'ble Chief Justice". It stated that all public interest litigations should be listed hereafter before a Division Bench. This office order was then applied with retrospective effect, to the petition. As a result, a reasoned judgment of the court was overruled by Justice Srikrishna retrospectively applying an office order. The petition was thereafter transferred to a specially assigned bench led by his lordship Justice Saraf who had earlier dismissed all petitions on this issue.

On 3 June, the High Court directed the petitioners to amend the writ petition to include all possible challenges. Further, it stated that it would examine all matters afresh. The High Court also directed Enron to place on record, audited

---

[127]Judgement passed by his lordship Justice Srikrishna in WP 2456 of 1996.

[128]*Ibid*: The "writ petition is essentially the other made under the Electricity Supply Act falling within Item 28 of Rule 18 of Chapter XVII of the Bombay High Court Appelate Side Rules, 1960". He also pointed out that "Rule 4 of the same chapter makes it clear that in doubtful cases, the only bar is that the single judge shall not make a final order on the application".

accounts of the US $20 million alleged to have been spent on the "education" of officials, failing which an "adverse inference" would be drawn. This direction of the court was carried out and in addition to the issues set out above, the petition was amended to raise several other issues.

The DPC asked for three weeks to reply and was granted the time. After this, in early July, the GoM asked for time and the matter was posted for the end of July. For all the concern shown by the DPC and the GoM for expediting the litigation, they were both responsible for a delay of over three months. Interestingly enough, the DPC neither placed these accounts before the court nor was an adverse inference ever drawn.

The petitioners put on record nearly 1800 pages of official records and documentation. Most of the documentation used in this book, was placed before the Hon'ble court.

A Short Account of the Proceedings

Confidentiality

The first round of discussions in court on 8 August 1996, was around the petitioners' challenge to the clearance given by the CEA on the basis of a set of confidential documents and communications between the government and Enron. Enron and the other respondents attempted to suppress the admission of all confidential documents as evidence, on the plea that the petitioners had obtained "purloined" documents. All respondents counsel (GoI, GoM, Enron, DPC, the CEA and the MSEB) objected to the petitioners' counsel, Shri Bhushan, from referring to any of these confidential documents. "It is in public interest that sanctity of government documents be maintained," said K.S. Cooper, counsel for the CEA.[129]

---

[129]Dalal, Sucheta and Somasekhar Sundaresan, "It is confidentiality vs. public interest", *Times of India*, 8 August 1996; Anon, "HC not buying Enron's secrecy argument", *Times of India*, 9 August 1996; (*contd.*)

Justice B.P. Saraf remarked: "There may be some public spirited government servants too". Since Cooper had initially alleged fabrication and then theft, Justice Saraf asked him if he denied the contents of the documents, saying "In that case, we are asking you to produce the originals to the court". Cooper admitted, "The copy is correct, there is no dispute on that". [130] K.K. Venugopal, arguing for Enron, told Shri Bhushan: "If you had fairly applied for these documents, we would have given them". Shri Bhushan pointed to the correspondence from the petitioners seeking the information, which was denied to them. Justice Saraf refused to reject outright consideration of documents claimed to be confidential and said that the court would look at the legal aspects of admissibility of documents at a later stage.[131]

In its suit of 1995, the GoM claimed that the earlier PPA had been "conceived in fraud" and that the contract "was against public policy". It was now faced with answering the obvious inference as to how it had contracted with the same corporation it had earlier accused of serious crimes. For example, it was claimed by GoM in its suit that tenders were not invited before the contract was awarded; the GoM was guilty of the very crime when it renegotiated the deal. The tariff was labelled prohibitively expensive, yet Phase I of the project was passed without any changes whatsoever. The arbitration and waiver of conditions precedent clauses were said to be "important constitutional issues on which ground alone, the agreement is void and/or inoperative in law". Yet the new agreement left them untouched. The GoM was therefore caught in a dilemma.

Mr Jethmalani, counsel for the GoM admitted to journalist

(*contd.*) Anon, "Enron: Right to knowledge versus state confidentiality", *Asian Age*, 9 August 1996.

[130] *Ibid.*

[131] *Ibid.*

Pranati Vora of the *Indian Express* that he held a retainership for Enron. He is quoted as saying, "Yes, they (Enron) did ask me for advice sometime earlier. I told this to the state government and the government's response was that there is no conflict of interest. So I have accepted the brief of the state". Advocate General C.J. Sawant's response was "I can only tell you that I have recommended that he be paid handsome fees". 'The ethical implications of running with the hares and hunting with the hounds were thus laid to rest'.[132]

The issue of *res judicata* was raised once more by the counsel for the GoM as well as the DPC before the division bench. The petitioners claimed that there was a material change in circumstances: the disclosure of the original PPA, the change in governments resulting in the disclosure of previously unavailable material to the public, the cancellation of the original PPA, the suit filed by the GoM and the various changes and additions to the project. Shri Shanti Bhushan, counsel for the petitioners, further argued that the present petition was being argued on different facts from that challenged in Ramdas Nayak petition. The CEA's concurrence was not an issue raised in the petition and, therefore, there could be no question of the bar of *res judicata*. In addition, Shanti Bhushan referred to standing case law, wherein the Supreme Court had held that violation of statute (in this case ESA) cannot be barred by *res judicata* and in any case, *res judicata* cannot apply when corruption is involved.

Shanti Bhushan then argued that the PPA was concluded without proper clearance from the CEA. The provisions of the Indian Electricity Act were not complied with, thereby rendering the CEA clearance illegal. Shri Bhushan alleged that the PPA was signed after bribes were offered to several officials. These officials then acted beyond their authority,

---

[132]Hutoxi Rustomfram in *The Lawyers Collective Magazine*, November 1996.

hence, the entire contract was void. Shri Bhushan also urged that electricity supply was something that affected all citizens and hence the CEA had to apply its own mind. The Act had not been amended so as to give power either to the state government or the union government or the finance ministry to negotiate the PPA with foreign providers of electricity. Lawyers for the respondents consistently raised the point that the issues had already been decided in earlier cases. Shri Bhushan referred to Supreme Court rulings which have laid down that this did not apply when corruption was involved. Numerous other irregularities were pointed out by Shri Bhushan, showing non-application of mind and corruption. Shri Bhushan further alleged that the CEA was forced to ignore the statutory procedures prescribed by the Indian Electricity Act.[133]

The next hurdle to be scaled was whether the earlier PPA was valid or whether a fresh one was negotiated. Atul Setalvad, representing the DPC claimed that the earlier PPA was not scrapped. Intriguingly, Ram Jethmalani, counsel for the GoM argued that it was in fact scrapped and renegotiated. Sunip Sen representing the petitioners argued that since the project was scrapped, as admitted by Jethmalani, the amended project was an entirely new one. (This was, in addition, admitted by both GoM as well as DPC when they had an earlier petition before Justice Vyas of the Bombay High Court dismissed on these grounds.) Therefore, the government should have followed its own prescription of inviting open bidding for the project. The entire arbitration hinged on the earlier contract being repudiated.

The agility of the GoM is noteworthy. Soon after it came into power, it cancelled the Dabhol project on the grounds of massive corruption and padding of costs. It then did a

---

[133]Anon, "Dabhol PPA 'has no legal clearance'", *Times of India*, 11 August 1996.

complete about-turn on the corruption issue. In its affidavit, the state has asserted that "even if there was an element of corruption, which is not easy to prove to the satisfaction of a judicial tribunal, the same would not necessarily invalidate the contract in as much as corruption is not one of the circumstances which vitiates a contract under the provisions of the Indian Contract Act".[134] Justice Saraf questioned the state government's lawyer on why they filed a suit against Enron alleging corruption when they did not have any substantial evidence of it. The government had consistently kept up the corruption charge to unilaterally cancel the Enron project and later to pre-empt arbitration proceedings in London. "On what basis did you file the plaint in the first place? The state government filing a suit is a serious thing," Justice Saraf said. "It was initially an irresponsible government," Ram Jethmalani admitted, "but later turned responsible". Justice Rane pointed to the specific allegations made in the plaint which had then been withdrawn and said it raised serious questions.[135] Interestingly, the bench had taken copies of the order withdrawing the government's suit for comparison, when the judges found that the copy served on the petitioner in the DPC's affidavit was not identical to that presented to the court.[136]

Shri Bhushan also demanded that Enron should furnish its accounts to the court showing how it had spent US $20 million, an amount that Enron official Linda Powers had said the company spent on educating Indian bureaucrats. "This was not part of the project cost. This was done to win support

---

[134]Affidavit dated July 25, 1996, made by Arvind Kumar, Deputy Secretary, Industries Energy and Labour Maharashtra in WP 2456 of 1996.

[135]Anon, "Enron Denies Pulling Strings for Contracts", *Times of India*, 22 July 1995.

[136]*Ibid.*

of the local people and the authorities". Justice Saraf, then said: "I hope these accounts are produced". Shri Bhushan remarked that "Judicial notice must be taken that in this country nothing moves except in a particular way. Has the US $20 million become US $30 million for the Maharashtra government to change its mind? Only the Enron representative will know best how this huge sum of money has been spent".[137]

The Defence

When Enron's advocate later began explaining Enron's stand on the Linda Powers statement, Justice Saraf told him that was not necessary, that the court was not insisting on seeing the accounts of expenditure of US $20 million. This was a major reprieve for Enron as the judge had earlier indicated that he would draw an adverse inference if accounts were not provided.[138]

Shri Jethmalani's rejoinder was that the CEA did not need to approve the tariff of a project as it was an aim of the government to formulate policy, not a regulator. It was further asserted by him that though the tariff was not strictly in accordance with the norms since it was accepted by the "prestigious" Foreign Investment Promotion Board, the deal was proceeded with. He also claimed that the CEA did not have to apply its mind "in matters such as tariff or the method of calculation as a condition precedent to granting concurrence". On the sticky issue of contracting with a corporation that the GoM had accused of fraud and corruption, Jethmalani's statement was succinct: "By scrapping the project we have made a political point and by

---

[137]Anon, "State Backtracks on Graft in Enron Case", *Times of India*, 8 August 1996; Anon, "Documents Reveal Confusion over Fuel Facility", *Times of India*, 8 August 1996.

[138]Anon, "Government fears political fallout of Enron case", *Times of India*, 17 August 1996.

reviewing it we have preserved the national interest". He is quoted in the *Times of India*, 16 August 1996, as saying, "if you strictly try to enforce new laws in all respects commerce will come to a standstill. Law should not be intractable and permit judicial interpretation". It was contended by the GoM that the suit was filed as a business strategy to obtain a favourable bargaining position and that Enron had sent feelers for re-negotiation even before the suit was filed. Jethmalani submitted that the object of the Munde Committee was also to create a "mood" for re-negotiation which came about on 31 August 1995.[139]

Ram Jethmalani, Counsel for the GoM, further contended that the allegations of corruption and fraud in the suit were averments and not admissions and that there was no need to furnish an affidavit from the Chief Minister. The only material available to the state government, he claimed, was the statement made by Linda Powers which they later found would not sustain the charge of corruption and therefore the PPA had to be re-negotiated in "public interest". At this juncture Justice Rane pointed out that apart from the Linda Powers statement there were other factors which led the state government to repudiate the earlier PPA, namely, lack of transparency, not inviting tenders, undue haste and that the PPA was against the people of Maharashtra.[140]

K.K. Venugopal, Counsel for Enron asserted that Enron was a victim in the present case. He contended that the "shifting stand" of the government of Maharashtra in the

---

[139]Anon, "State had no power to negotiate Enron PPA, High Court told", *Indian Express*, 10 August 1996; Anon, "CITU brings forex outflow at DPC under microscope", *Economic Times*, 13 August 1996; Anon, "State cannot re-negotiate PPA: CITU", *Asian Age*, 13 August 1996. Hutoxi Rustomfram in *The Lawyers Collective Magazine*, November 1996.
[140]*Ibid.*

matter of repudiation of the PPA and then renegotiation, should not affect the validity of the PPA.[141]

The respondents' counsels also contradicted themselves in court. According to the counsel for the DPC, A.M. Setalvad, the original PPA had not been terminated but had been modified and some of its terms re-negotiated. According to the state of Maharashtra's counsel, Ram Jethmalani, the PPA had been scrapped and a new agreement had been negotiated. The State had given directions to the MSEB to stop further work on the Dabhol project and the board had complied with this request of the State.[142]

The Petitioner's Counter Arguments

On 17 August 1996, Shri Bhushan declared that the suit filed by the state was an admission made by a party to the legal proceeding and could be used against the party making such an admission. The burden of proving the earlier statement wrong lay upon the state. Thereafter, the court requested the CM to file a detailed affidavit detailing all the facts and circumstances. The final arguments of the petitioners finished on Saturday, 17 August. Shri Bhushan again demanded an explanation of the US $20 million, which Enron's lawyers could not explain. Shri Bhushan argued that the GoM and the Chief Minister had acted in an irresponsible manner, for according to them, since it was difficult to prove allegations of corruption against Enron, the State had tried to re-negotiate the PPA. Shri Bhushan wondered whether political compulsion was the reason for the re-negotiation, or it was dishonesty. He pointed out that the re-negotiation started only after Rebecca Mark met the Shiv Sena chief Bal Thackeray. Shri Bhushan suggested that the Chief Minister

---

[141]*Ibid.*

[142]Anon, "State had no power to negotiate Enron PPA, High Court told", *Indian Express*, 10 August 1996.

or any other responsible person should file an affidavit explaining how allegations of corruption came to be made in the suit filed by the State, repudiating the earlier PPA, and how the suit came to be withdrawn.[143]

Finally, Sunip Sen arguing for the petitioners, contended that the re-negotiated PPA was a substantial departure from the original PPA in respect of the total generating power capacity, the reduced capital cost, as also the change of original fuel oil or distillate to naphtha. Sen urged that any substantial modification or alteration to the PPA had to be re-notified in the Gazette, and the whole process had to be undergone afresh, after calling for objections and waiting for a period of 60 days and submission of the scheme for approval of the CEA under the mandatory provision of Section 32 of the ESA.[144]

The High Court's Direction

The division Bench then directed the Chief Minister and the Deputy Chief Minister (who holds the energy portfolio) of Maharashtra to file affidavits stating the reasons for scrapping the Dabhol power project and then re-negotiating it. The affidavits would also explain why the State government had leveled corruption charges against DPC and still opted for re-negotiation.[145]

On 3 September 1996, the chief minister of Maharashtra filed an affidavit that was deliberately false. He affirmed on oath, that all the allegations of fraud, misrepresentation and corruption made in the suit, were made on the "basis of

---

[143]Anon, "CITU wants Joshi to file affidavit", *Asian Age*, 18 August 1996.

[144]8. Anon, "When did CEA clear Enron's project?", *Times of India*, 12 August 1996; Anon, "New Enron Deal is No Different, HC told", *Times of India*, 13 August 1996.

[145]See note 141.

newspaper reports". He maintained that "during the pendency of the suit renegotiations were carried on with the company and the government succeeded in getting favourable terms which included reduction in capital cost" among other reliefs. Finally, the suit was withdrawn. He went on to assert that "the various steps taken by my government, namely, reviewing the project, cancelling the project, filing a suit, renegotiating the terms and conditions of the project and withdrawing the suit were all done in a bonafide manner in the larger interest of the consumers and the people of Maharashtra".

The court instructed the Advocate General to incorporate a new line as part of the affidavit while commenting on the corruption issue. The Bench instructed the court clerk to add the words that the allegations of bribery and corruption made against Enron in various newspapers were 'without basis'.[146]

The Petitioners Prohibited from Replying to this Perjurious Affidavit

The High Court prohibited the petitioners from replying to the CM's perjurious affidavit. The court took the affidavit on file and declined the petitioners' request to file a written reply to it or even to put up oral arguments. Justice Saraf observed, "There is a limit to which we can go on taking papers on record". You may give more written submission to the court but we will not look at them; and further, "we will get them sealed and simply keep it in the records. If we go on arguing this can go on for ever".[147] The media responded with some

---

[146]Anon, "Charges against DPC 'without base', admits Joshi", *Economic Times*, 3 September 1996; Anon, "Shock over CM's affidavit on Enron", *Times of India*, 4 September 1996; Anon, "Joshi passes Enron buck to media", *Times of India*, 3 September 1996.

[147]*Times of India*, 9 September, 1996.

anger but in a couple of days the indignation appeared to have died a natural death.

The complete testimony of Linda Powers was available when the suit was filed and has been specifically referred to in the plaint. Further, the suit filed by the GoM gave specific illustrations and examples of fraud and misrepresentation, based on the documentary record, a comprehensive list of which was annexed to the suit. The GoM's plaint contained 38 enclosures.[148] No mention of press reports was made or documentation of press clippings furnished. The affidavit also does not refer, inter alia, to the substantial infringement of public policy and interest; breach of norms and propriety etc. that had motivated cancellation.

The High Court's Judgment

On 2 December 1996, the High Court delivered its judgment. The High Court noted that

> This case has highlighted to the people as to how even after 50 years of independence, political considerations outweigh the public interest and the interest of the State and to what extent the Government only can go to justify its actions and not only before the public but even before the Courts of law.

It noted that the renegotiated contract was shrouded in as much secrecy as the original contract and observed that Enron conquered much more than it did earlier.

However, it simply allowed the matter to rest there. It dismissed the petition on the basis of its judgement passed in

---

[148]Suit filed by the GoM; annexures included correspondence between the state and Enron, government notifications, arbitration notices, annual reports of Enron, Bombay High Court's earlier order and a report by the National Working Group on Power, among other documents.

the Ramdas Nayak case i.e., on the basis of the doctrine of *res judicata*.

The High Court in its judgment did not deal with the challenges on merit dismissing it on technical grounds (*res judicata*) rather on the merits of the petitioners' submissions and evidence. The case in seeking judicial review had been confined to questions of legality, rationality and propriety of the decision-making process. The high court did not address these key questions at all.

Interestingly enough, none of the evidences used in this book was taken into account in the judgment nor is there any mention in the judgment of the fact that all the evidences were placed before the court.

The key and sole issue of whether or not the project had a valid clearance under the provisions of the Electricity (Supply) Act and whether the CEA had failed in its statutory duties is not addressed at all in the judgment. All other issues raised by the petitioners were also not dealt with in the judgement.

On 2 May 1997, the Supreme Court of India, in what appears to be one of the strangest decisions in recent times, did not allow any arguments on the issues raised by the above judgment, the documentary evidence and on the critical question of the clearance by the CEA. The Supreme Court deleted all but one of the answering parties including the Government of India, the CEA and Enron, i.e., neither the CEA nor the MSEB and Enron are answerable in this case. Effectively, the decision amounts to an honorable exoneration.

It went on to limit the scope of the judicial examination to the changing stances of the Maharashtra government and appointed an *amicus curiae* to help the court. However, till date, there has been no hearing on the matter inspite of repeated requests to the court. The matter is still pending (October 1998) before the Supreme Court, limited to the changing stances of the Maharashtra government.

17

Epilogue

The sordid saga narrated in these pages is still not complete and the last chapter in this is yet to be written. The issues ranging from the capacity of the MSEB to pay these enormous sums of moneys, the effect on consumers, to the effect on Maharashtra's economy in the not too distant future have yet to surface. Consider one aspect—if all goes as per schedule, the MSEB will be paying three private parties something to the tune of eight thousand crore a year for twenty years. These payments of course will keep on increasing because of the multiplicity of built-in indices. This sum of money will represent a substantial strain on the state's economy. The only redeeming feature, if it could be termed as one, is that neighbouring states like Karnataka and Gujarat will be in no better position.

It is my contention that an outgoing of this magnitude is not sustainable. The geese will come home to roost. In a few years, present day Bihar will look like the epitome of fiscal health as compared to Maharashtra.

At this stage I would like to make my personal views clear. I do not believe that the problem is with Enron per se. In fact, having said all that I have, I must also confess to a sneaking admiration for a remarkable opponent, for securing the deal of the century. Enron did what most business houses would have done to secure such a deal.

I think that, by and large, we do not accept responsibility for ourselves and instead prefer to take the softer alternative of blaming the 'other'. This could mean 'outside forces', or the usual gang of suspects—the IMF, World Bank and GATT or Enron itself. However, in my opinion, the problem lies mostly with us—the Indian nation state of India and all that term represents or should represent. At the core of this problem lies our inability to deal with or look after our own interests and to take respnsibility for our actions or the lack thereof.

Consider for a start, in the events described in the book, the complete and total abdication of even a semblance of what could be construed as governance. There was a complete failure of every conceivable institutional structure—the government, the press, courts as well as of institutions—constitutional, statutory or those emerging from the executive. The number of institutions that were subverted, bypassed, simply ignored, or who chose to look the other way is almost unbelievable. These include the CEA, the MoP, the judiciary (from the High Court to the Supreme Court), even obscure departments of the GoM like the Ports Department, the MSEB, the law ministry at both the Centre and in the State, the IDBI, the GoM, the Finance department, Central and State Cabinets, the department of Industry and Energy in Maharashtra, the MoF, the press, two all-party parliamentary committees, the Auditor General of the country, the Accountant General of Maharashtra—the list goes on.

The Next Round of Scams

One salvo in the next round of scams has already been fired—the so-called rationalisation of the SEBs; the attempt to make them more efficient by breaking them up into independent distribution, transmission and generation companies. Purportedly induced by the dictates of the World Bank, we have already made a hash of it. The 'privatisation' of the SEBs involves the sale of assets worth several tens of thousand of crores, needless to say, for a song.

Take one of the most obvious cases—the Torrent group's acquisition of the Ahmedabad and Surat Electricity companies in Gujarat. The group acquired assets at less than a tenth of their market value from the government. All safeguards that existed were rendered ineffectual. Several finance department notes were overruled; a court order stipulating that the government should inform the court if they sold any more shares to the Torrent group, was merrily ignored and public interest litigants "settled" a public interest litigation privately.

One minor saving grace comes to mind. Contingent liabilities that the SEBs carry might make this process more difficult. To illustrate, the MSEB's contingent liabilities stemming out of its contractual obligations with IPP's are substantially more than the state's GDP's. Unless the state takes these massive liabilities upon itself (which it may very well do), no private party would dream of dealing with contingent liabilities of this magnitude. Nonetheless, smaller versions (e.g. "privatising" smaller local areas) remains open e.g., highly industrialised belts in Maharashtra (which are MSEB's most profitable customers) like the Thane Belapur belt, the Navi Mumbai belt and smaller parts of the industrialised corridor may very well occur, i.e., the SEB sells off its assets (physical as well as distribution) to private parties for a fraction of their actual worth.

Most of the ills that plague the power system are amenable to being reversed rather trivially—from metering (over 40% of the electricity produced in the country is not metered) to energy efficient devices, administrative and fiscal reform etc.

However, the path of emulating a different system without even an iota of understanding of the underlying basis of that system seems to be our usual fate. Institutions like the CEA have been completely emasculated while the new regulatory commission model is somewhat akin to closing the stable doors after the horse has bolted. The subversion of the law has graduated from the farcical to the tragic. For example, when the CEA refused to carry out the diktat of a secretary in the Ministry of Power, all salaries in the CEA were stopped for a full month in January of 1998!

Lastly, the completely unequal terms on which these processes have taken place merits a special mention. What I allude to, is the specificity of state intervention or non-intervention for that matter. In this country the idea of development is largely specific to a class of population and it is operationally defined and used for the specific class. This is in deliberate exclusion of a set of people who do not matter and are considered absolutely irrelevant in the process. The Indian state and all that flows from that, whether it is Reliance Industries or the most ordinary citizen, has internalised and integrated this concept totally. The state apparatus has been directly responsible. The victims at the altar do not matter in any reckoning. A single colonial law—which we have not bothered to alter at all over the last 50 years—the process of acquisition of land and the Land Acquisition Act (1894)—has been responsible for the deprivation of millions. It violates a range of what constitutes fundamental human rights—from the right to live, the right to livelihood, a right to protection from being forcibly displaced, on terms that are an affront and an abuse of the powers of the state, the right to be treated on equal terms. A century has passed, but this legal and social anomaly has not changed; in fact it has worsened. The amendments to the Act, proposed in 1998, or the related acts for land acquisition e.g., the MIDC Act, are even more draconian. If one is espousing "free market" policies, the least that could be done is to let the companies that want to, say, purchase land, do so directly from the affected people on terms that are acceptable to both—the buyer and the seller—without the state using the might of all the forces at its disposal in favour of the buyer.

Post Script, August 1999

Monsoon is traditionally a lean period for electricity demand, but the measures that the MSEB has undertaken to absorb the electricity from the DPC border on the criminal. These include not buying between 200 and 250 MW of power from the Tatas at Rs 1.80/unit and backing off some of its own units at Chandrapur (at Rs 1.20/unit). The direct loss to MSEB on this account amounts to Rs 460 crore a year. Lastly, the Nationalist Congress Party (Sharad Pawar's latest outfit) had the temerity to issue a statement that they would renegotiate the contract they came to power.

And, the show has just begun!

Appendix 1

The Enron Oil Saga

ONGC had explored huge tracts in offshore India. Based on this, after the preliminary rounds of semi-random discovery at great expense, it had discovered fields with a confirmed potential amounting in the $100 billion dollar range. These included the off-shore Gujarat (Mukta Panna), the Tapti river basin, off-shore Andhra Pradesh and other places. ONGC started preliminary work on some of these fields. It spent Rs 500 crore on developing the Panna-Mukta oil fields. This does not include the money spent on the process of discovering the fields in the first place. ONGC started oil production from the wells and was producing about 4 million barrels of oil a year from them. ONGC was and is being paid administered prices.

Opening Up

In 1991 pursuant to the conditionalities attached to the WB loan to the ONGC, the government of India decided to invite private sector participation in the oil and gas sector. On 29.6.91 a note on the matter was drafted by one Ashok Chandra of the Ministry of Petroleum and Natural Gas (MoPG). This note stated that an acceptable middle path would be to make the proposal of the World Bank contingent upon necessity, i.e. as and when necessary, the Government if it so deemed appropriate could invite private sector participation into the petroleum sector. A formal "Formulation of Policy on opening up the petroleum sector on account of World Bank Pressure" was thereafter seen and approved by the then minister of petroleum. This formulation was essentially the one drafted by Shri Ashok Chandra, i.e. an appropriate formulation of words that would not irrevocably commit or bind the government. However this formulation was overruled on express instructions of the then Prime Minister and Finance Secretary who instructed Shri Chandra to make the formulation irrevocably binding on the government. Upon being overruled, Shri Chandra then sought and received the signature of the Prime Minister Shri Narsimha Rao on the file.

The New Policy

Thereafter, the government not only allowed ONGC and Oil India Ltd. (OIL) to enter into joint ventures with private parties, but, strangely enough, went much further. It decided to lease out the oil and gas fields that had already been discovered and developed by ONGC and OIL to joint ventures between private sector parties and ONGC/OIL. In any case, the ministry thereafter drafted a policy for inviting private sector participation. Specific extracts from the policy are reproduced below.[1]

> Projects for the development of the Mukta and Panna oil fields in the Western offshore have already been approved by Government. While ONGC has taken action to implement the projects and the various components of the projects are being set up by them on the basis of global tendering, this process is severely handicapped due to lack of competition in these tenders. It is, therefore, proposed to offer these two fields for development on a joint venture basis...
>
> On receipt of offers, the comparative economics of developing these fields on joint venture basis vis-à-vis ONGC/OIL developing these fields on their own would be examined and thereafter a final decision would be taken on the development of each field on a joint venture basis.

This policy was developed after having sought and received the concurrence of among others the Finance and Revenue departments. Thereafter, this policy was approved by the Cabinet Committee on Economic Affairs (the CCEA).

At this juncture, it may be relevant to appreciate that in the normal course, developed and producing oil fields are almost never handed over to other parties. The discovery of oil/gas fields is the most difficult part of the process. Conventionally (in the USA for example) the federal government lets out acreage. i.e. a certain number of acres in a particular area to private bidders. The bidder undertakes all risk. All expenses including the process of gathering physical data from the field, analysing, trial wells etc. are borne by the bidders. Needless to say that this process involves considerable amount of risk and expenses.

The Policy is Violated

In specific and explicit violation of the policy, for reasons that are unclear, the ministry omitted to do an analysis of basic bidding parameters like

---

[1]Note dated 7.6.92, drafted by H.C. Gupta, Jt. Sec. MoPG in File No. 0-19018-36-91-ONG-DO.VI. The note is titled "Sub-Participation by ONGC/OIL in Joint Verntures with private parties for Development of discovered oil and gas fields and in enhanced oil recovery (EOR) schemes."

comparative cost economics, reserve estimates, bidding procedure and even the criteria for evaluation of bids was not carried out. Neither was the comparative cost economics of a Joint Venture (JV) vs ONGC itself developing the fields was not carried out. It simply issued tender notice inviting private parties to participate in the joint development of *inter alia* the Panna Mukta fields. The notice inviting bids set the last date for receiving tenders as 31 December 1992. The notice also set out the amounts of reserve in the Panna Mukta fields as 31.5 MMT (million metric tonnes).

The Government Invites Bids

On 31 March, 1993, the government retrospectively extended the last date for receipt of the bids to 31 March, 1993. As far as the author is aware, the consortium that was finally awarded the Mukta-Panna fields (consortium of Reliance Industries and Enron Corporation) had not made a bid by 31 December, 1992. In fact, Reliance Industries had applied with relatively unknown and minor companies (Olympic Oil of New York and another company).

It is critical to note at the relevant time, neither Reliance nor Enron Corporation have any experience of operating off shore oil and gas fields. Enron would not have made it through the preliminary technical qualifications stage by itself. Therefore, this story like most stories in this saga ought to have ended there itself.

Evaluation of the Bids

The bids were not opened in public nor in the presence of the bidders as is the normal governmental practice. No record of officials present at the time of opening the bids was maintained. The comparative statements of the original versus the revised bids were neither authenticated nor dated.

The amount of reserves kept dwindling during the process of "evaluation of bids". ONGC's own feasibility report gave 31.35 MMT as the amount of recoverable oil reserves. The tender documents issued to the bidders mention the amount of recoverable reserves to be 31.5 MMT. The evaluation of the bids was done by assuming the amount of recoverable reserves to be 14.5 MMT.

The chairman of ONGC, resigned his job to join Reliance, i.e., the same firm whose bids were in the middle of being evaluated.

Thereafter on 27 March 1993 one Mr Misra of Reliance Industries wrote to Mr Ramani of MoPG inter alia requesting the "composition of the negotiating team" of the government in the negotiations with various bidders.

On 24 June 1993 Mr Ramani, MoPG wrote to Dr Aggarwal (Ministry of Law), Ms Murali (Ministry of Finance) and Mr R.B. Mehrotra (Member Exploration, ONGC) requesting them to attend the meeting with RIL and Enron to "discuss the strategy for negotiations".

All of them also were members of the negotiating team. The negotiating teams meet with RIL-Enron between 28 June and 2 July, 1993.

Mr R.B. Mehrotra joined the consortium a few months later. Dr Agrawal's wife was allotted a petrol pump from the petroleum minister's discretionary quota in September 1993.

In October 1993, a committee of secretaries consisting of the finance secretary, the petroleum secretary and revenue secretary decided to hand the fields. Panna-Mukta was awarded to the Enron-Reliance Joint Venture and Ravva to the Videocon-Command consortium.

Economics of the Contracts

Consider one aspect of the contract signed. For reasons best known to the government, the government has agreed to pay the consortium prices well in excess than paid by the government to ONGC. For discovered, developed and producing fields this is unprecedented.

Gas Pricing

The history of this makes interesting reading.

On 22 December, 1994, Mr Ramani of the MoPG, prepares a note. This note (at page 6) discusses gas price to be paid to RIL-Enron. In the note, Mr Ramani makes the admission that these prices are "higher than current market prices". He goes on to further admit that these prices are even "higher" than gas price offered to Videocon (whose contract was signed at about the same time). The Government agency (The Gas Authority of India— GAIL) would be purchasing the gas at price higher than current administered price.

Thereafter he goes on to suggest that as a result, "some mechanism be put in place" to "ensure that economics of GAIL is not affected". This could be done either by providing an "explicit subsidy" to GAIL or letting GAIL charge "market price" to its own consumers i.e. prices which would presumably be higher than the purchase prices by GAIL and perhaps therefore market prices.

On the same day, 22 December, 1994, the important note has been finalised by Mr Ramani. Thereafter, on 22nd December, 1994 itself, the note is received, read and approved by Director (EC), Najeeb Jung. He justifies the higher pricing and submits for approval. Presumably after having received his approval, the file then moves to the JS (E) who then approves it.

Thereafter, the file flying through the corridors of the ministry, reaches the office of the Joint Secretary and financial advisor to MoPG at "1310 hrs" on 22 December, 1994, for his "immediate concurrence as contract is to be signed at 1330". This gentleman obviously could not "study" the note and goes on to sign "Concurred as recommended by DS (F)".

Presumably the note had also passed through the hands of the DS (F) on the same day. Assuming it took the JS and FA a few minutes to sign and pass on the file to the Secretary, MoPG. He goes through it and signs it. The signature is dated 22 December 1994.

The Hon'ble Minister then receives the file. The Hon'ble minister's signature is dated 22 December 1994.

One might recollect that the file had reached the JS and FA at 13.10 hrs.

The Contract is signed at 13.30 hours on 22 December, 1994.

For the record, the consortium is being paid $2.97 to $3.11/MMBTU of gas. This is 50 per cent more than the price received by Enron in the USA and 230 per cent more than its fields in the West Indies.[2]

Oil Prices

The prices paid by the government in purchasing oil from its own oil fields. For the first three months of 1997. The Enron/Reliance Joint

---

[2]Average prices that were received by Enron from various fields are set out in Form 10Q submitted by Enron and Gas Inc. (EO&G) to the Securities and Exchange Commission (SEC) in the United States of America (USA) for various quarters between 1993 and 1997.

Venture was paid \$ 22.99[3] while in the same period i.e. in the first three months of 1997.

(i) The average FOB price of all US crude imports was \$ 19.13[4]

(ii) The average FOB price of Brent crude was \$ 21.13[5]

(iii) The average price received by Enron Oil from its fields in the West Indies was \$ 18.86[6]

(iv) The price paid to ONGC was \$ 13[7].

Severe Discrimination between National Oil Companies and the JV

Relative Economics of Pricing

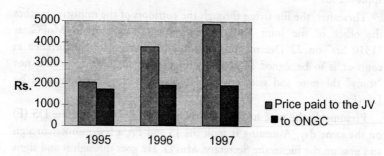

Net price paid to ONGC in 1997	Rs 1941 a tonne or \$ 7.14 a barrel
Net price paid to the JV in 1997	Rs 4867 a tonne @ \$ 22.99[8] a barrel
Net price paid to ONGC in 1996 (after 1/4/96)	Rs 1941 a tonne or \$ 7.70 a barrel
Net price paid to the JV in 1996	Rs 3796 a tonne @ \$ 20.17 a barrel
Net price paid to ONGC in 1995	Rs 1741 a tonne or \$ 7.26 a barrel
Net price paid to the JV in 1995	Rs 2807 a tonne @ \$ 16.81 a barrel

Retrospective Defences

The GoI four years later, in October 1997, during the course of a Public Interest Petition challenging the award of the oil fields to the

---

[3]Form 10Q submitted by EO&G to the SEC on 15/4/97 for the 1st quarter of 1997.

[4]The US department of energy.

[5]Dow Jones reporting service.

[6]Form 10Q submitted by EOG to the SEC, USa for the 1st quarter of 1997.

[7]Annual Report of ONGC, 1997.

[8]In the first three months @ \$ 22.99 a barrel and exchange rate of Rs. 36 to a dollar.

Reliance-Enron Consortium claimed that the criteria for awarding the tenders was on the highest NPV of the net government 'take' as given by various bidders. The bid evaluation criteria were not included in the bid invitation. The NPV analysis was purportedly done on the basis of the quoted Operating and Capital expenditure submitted by various bidders. However the PSC which the government signed has, not included as a firm commitment, (i) guarantees for committed production levels, (ii) nor has OPEX been included in the PSC.

The issue of past costs is not addressed by the government, in spite of its own admonitions to bidders at the time of "negotiations" to reimburse ONGC for its admitted expenditure of at least Rs 500 crore. In current terms the total costs incurred by ONGC amount to a figure far higher than that. Additional costs by the ONGC to the tune of Rs 234 crore are not considered at all.

The government claims that "the signature and production bonuses were meant to compensate the risk taken by ONGC in discovering the fields". As per the PSC, the signature bonus was made to ONGC in consideration of the right to commence and carry out exploration and drilling activity as an existing mining lease holder. Thereby, the signature bonus that is claimed to be a reimbursement of past costs, is in no way related to past costs at all.

The "proposed" "signature bonus" in any case, amounts to a paltry Rs 12.6 crore, presumably payable when the contractor deems fit. This amount is incommensurable with the amounts spent by ONGC in the exploration and development of the fields. The "proposed" "production bonuses" are due only in the 8th and 14th year. The NPV of the "proposed" signature bonuses and the "production bonuses" would amount to only a very insignificant fraction of the actual and admitted costs incurred by ONGC. In fact they amount to nearly zero.

The Fraudulent Payments

The government of India, in a sworn affidavit,[9] claimed to have "authorised payments of $ 18.869 per barrel in the month of June 1997". There was no production of crude in June 1997.[10] In a mandatory

---

[9]Affidavit of the GoI, in WP 3020 of 1997 (Delhi High Court).

[10]In a writ petition filed by Enron in the Bombay High Court, being Original Side Writ Petition No. 524 of 1997, Enron stated that the operations in Panna-Mukta oil fields would shut down around April 1997 for commissioning of the installed process complex.

filing made by Enron Oil in the USA[11] Enron reported that there was no revenue received from the Panna/Mukta oilfields in the 2nd quarter of 1997 i.e. for the months of April, May and June of 1997, Enron oil did not receive any payments from the sale of oil from the Mukta and Panna fields.

When these facts were published in the media, the government simply went on to claim that there was a typographical error in the affidavit in 4 different places and went on to file a fresh affidavit stating that the example was a hypothetical one.

The Overall Loss

The overall loss to the public exchequer on account of the prices paid in the Panna-Mukta deal together with the fact that we will be buying gas for the Dabhol project from the same company—Enron, amounts to at least $ 6 billion dollars. This is a minimum estimation. In all likelihood, the loss will be considerably more and thereby hangs a tale...

---

[11]Form 10Q submitted by EOG to the SEC, USA for the 2nd quarter of 1997.

Appendix 2

A number of issues have not been dealt with in the book. Among others, the obvious question—what, if anything can be done at this stage? Additionally, a number of minor episodes, need to be alluded to. Some of these episodes include, an analysis of the corporate structure of DPC, MSEB's own analysis of the tariff versus what was represented to the public, how the tariff was accorded a 'clearance' a year after the PPA was signed, the role of the press, the role played by certain academics, specificities on what can be done versus what was and is being done, the IDBI's analysis of the project, what happened to Enron in Pakistan, the role of obscure departments of the GoM.

No Way Out

As far as I can tell, there is no way out. To illustrate, consider the hypothetical case that a future government finding it impossible to pay the several thousand crores a year, would want to try and wriggle out the contract. This will prove to be well impossible. The present government have made this or for that matter most, courses of action impossible to sustain on any legal grounds anywhere. The present government had taken all conceivable grounds in trying to negate the contract. However, since they went on to say, on oath, that they were wrong and did not have any basis whatsoever in taking grounds like infringement of public policy, fraud, corruption, misrepresentation and breach of statue. Any future course of action would have to traverse this rather impossible course.

The Corporate Structure of DPC Unlimited

The DPC is a private company with unlimited liability incorporated in India. The corporate structure of the DPC is quite unusual. The share holding by Enron Corporation in the DPC is through a network of at least six holding companies. These companies are in turn incorporated in various off shore locations in a series of complex cross holdings.

Interestingly enough, for most parts the DPC is a shell company. Almost everything comes from subsidiary companies of the parent companies from maintenance to gas. A vast network of Enron subsidiaries supply everything to the DPC from gas worth two thousand or so crores a year to other subsidiaries supplying items valued at a few crores. GE, another shareholder, is supplying equipment valued at a few thousand crores. The third partner, Bechtel, is constructing the plant, supposedly at a cost of two thousand crores.

The IDBI's Analysis of the Project

This too involves a number of interesting episodes. However, I will limit it to two. IDBI's first round of analysis had indicted that the project as over invoiced substantially and a number of other details. It appears that the bank on account of these and other problems, could not fund the project. However, mysteriously enough about a month later, in another meeting, the problems are not alluded to and the bank goes on to finance the project and also guarantee a large portion of the foreign loans. The second story is that among other issues that emerged from a break up of total project costs under various heads was a 550 crore head roughly amounting to miscellaneous. It is to be noted that this was for the first phase that was supposedly costing a total of Rs 2800 crores then.

Certain Academics

Not unlike most people who were against the project, this well known academic was vehemently against the project. His opposition was on economic grounds as well as others (e.g. the guarantees etc.). A number of articles in the press before a certain juncture in time illustrate this stand. Rather abruptly, a complete about turn occurred in his publicly stated position, when, overnight, he suddenly saw a great deal of merit in the project. This change of heart occurred after two visitors dropped by in his office.

MSEB's Analysis of the Tariff

MSEB's analysis of the tariff indicated that the starting tariff at the then prevailing price of oil ad exchange rate, would be no less than Rs 3.85. This would involve payments to Enron of Rs 1380 crores in the very first year of the first phase. The public or for that matter the parliament was informed by the then Hon'ble minister that the tariff would be Rs 2.40. These are non trivial errors. Each paisa represents nearly 20 crores in payments.

The Role of the Press

This is one key issue that the author wishes to apologise for not going into some details. Nonetheless the following will have to suffice. The first issue is that of a large section of the press as flag waving loyalists—more loyal than the king. Manmohan Singh had the remarkable grace and perhaps almost unthinkable in this day to admit in public that he had been wrong. Unfortunately that cannot be said about the vehement loyalists in the large sections of the press. On the other hand, there were a number of remarkable individuals in the press who did have the courage, the intelligence and dedication to write and present the other side of the case. These include sections of the *Times of India,* the *Hindu, Businessline, Frontline, The Hindustan Times, Outlook,* and the *Statesman* in the mainstream English media. On another vein altogether, perhaps the reader will remember the nearly daily stream of articles, columns and reporting that emerged from the pages of the *Indian Express.* These ranged from a series of articles by Bharat Bhushan on how the project was "cleared"—perhaps one of the finest examples of investigative reportage in the last decade or more—or consider the weekly columns covering Enron by R.N. Bhaskar, the regular series of stories by Raghunandan Dhar and a few other intrepid reporters.

Did the reader notice an sudden overnight transition?

Appendix 3

The Amnesty International Report (Extracts) "The Enron Project in Maharashtra"

The report, released in June 1997, covers a six month period between January and June 1997.

A battalion of the State Reserve Police, stationed on the site of the power plant, the local police and company security guards have all been implicated in the violations. Amnesty International is concerned at the collusion of the police with those supporting the construction of the project, which has increased the vulnerability of the protesters to human rights violations.

According to information received by Amnesty International, DPC has sought to provide security for its property and employees in two ways. Reports indicate that prior to the protest of 30 January 1997, the company sub-contracted private security guards from local security companies, but that following this, security guards have been directly employed by the DPC. In addition, DPC reportedly requested the state government to provide police protection in the aftermath of protests which took place on 30 January 1997.

Following this request, the DPC allegedly entered into a contractual security arrangement with the Government of Maharashtra, and a battalion of 100 State Reserve Police (SRP), which was deployed on the site. Reports indicate that although the SRP personnel continued to be paid by the state government, the DPC paid the state authorities for the additional battalion at a cost of Rs 125 ($US 3.50) per day for each police constable. Reports also indicate that two sub-inspectors in charge of the battalion stationed at the DPC site remained within the chain of command of the state police and worked in tandem with the sub-inspector of Guhagar taluka (district sub-division) police station.

Amnesty International is concerned that the use of force in the context of the Enron protests has not been in proportion to the seriousness of the crime, and that excessive force has been used, in a routine manner. The organization is not aware of injury to any law enforcement official, nor of any medical treatment received by such an official, in contrast to the pattern of injuries received by the protesters. The police, including the Special Reserve Police on the site of the company, have routinely used excessive force to suppress the protests and whilst arresting villagers and protesters, and those arrested have been held in conditions amounting to cruel, inhuman and degrading treatment. Some of these incidents are detailed here.

During the arrests that took place on 3 June 1997, after the arrival of 135 police and SRP personnel in the village, a 23 year-old woman in the late stages of pregnancy, Dhanashree Janardhaan Padyal, was beaten. Others who sustained injuries did not seek medical help because of the fear of police reprisals. Another woman, Sugandha Vasudev Bhalekar—a 24 year old housewife who was three months pregnant at the time of her arrest on 3 June—testified to the Judicial Magistrate, on 9 June:

"at arond 5 in the morning when I was in the bathroom, several male police with batons in their hands forcibly entered the house and started beating members of (my) family who were asleep…Being terrified, I told them from inside the bathroom that I was taking a bath and that I would come out after wearing my clothes. I asked them to call for women police in the meantime and to ask them to wait near the door. But without paying any attention to my requests, the policemen forcibly opened the door and dragged me out of the house into the police van parked on the road. (While dragging me) the police kept beating me on my back with batons. The humiliation meted out to the other members of my family was similar to the way I was humiliated…my one and a half year old daughter held on to me but the police kicked her away."

Reports indicate that she was targeted for attack by the police because husband, Baba Bhalekar, was a known leader of the protests.

Of the 26 women arrested, 25 were held in one room of 150 square feet with a washing area and toilet at one end and steel mesh at the other, overlooked by a constable. According to the PUCL team who visited the police lock-up on 7 June: "There was no light or fan…The entire room stank". Amnesty International believes that the conditions in the Chiplun police station lock-up amount to cruel, inhuman and degrading treatment.

On 17 February 1997, a member of the SRP reportedly assaulted Sanjay Pawar, a road maintenance supervisor after he requested a Major of the SRP not to drive past his worksite at high speed. The supervisor, a handicapped youth, reportedly received an injury to his skull. Sanjay Pawar was later arrested on 20 February, and charged under Section 341 (punishment for wrongful restraint), 353 (assault or criminal force to deter public servant from discharge of his duty) and 504 (intentional insult with intent to provoke breach of the peace) of the IPC on a charge of attempting to assault an SRP official, which Amnesty International considers to be false.

On 30 January 1997, over three thousand people gathered to protest in a dharna and a morcha at the three gates of the site of the Enron project. As protesters gathered, police reportedly began pushing protesters and without warning began charging them with lathis. Several people including 17 women were beaen and several women were forcibly pushed into a police van. Reports suggest that approximately 450 people were arrested and taken to the town of Chiplun, and a total of 679 people were charged under sections 37(1) and (3) and section 135 of the Bombay Police Act taluka of Ratnagiri district, Maharashtra and has to the temporary imprisonment of hundreds of people. Those arrested were reportedly kept for several hours without food and water, and were finally released in batches on 30 and 31 January.

The previous day, a delegation of seven members of the Sangharsh Samiti and two villagers who visited Guhagar taluka police station, were arrested under section 151 of the CRPC. They had gone to ask the police to take appropriate action "to prevent certain vested interests from creating violence on the following day of the satyagraha". The delegation went to the police following a tour of the local police station, in which the Deputy Superintendent of Police allegedly toured the affected villages, threatening that the police would resort to firing if considered necessary, on the day of the planned dharna.

Police collusion

The vulnerable position of villagers protesting against the Eron project has been reinforced by the collusion of local police with those promoting the construction of the project. Members of the SRP, seconded to the DPC, have been implicated in human rights violations (see above) and on a number of occasions the police have refused to register complaints made by villagers against construction workers and other supporters of the project.

In Kathalwadi on 1 April, four supporters of the project reportedly attacked some of the anti-Enron group with swords, acid and soda bottles. The next day the police officer on duty at the local police station refused to accept the complaint of those attacked on the grounds that a complaint had already been filed by supporters of the project. As a result of this earlier complaint, 21 men and women from Kathalwadi were arrested by police on chares including "attempt to murder". They were remanded to judicial custody for almost three weeks—19 were released on 19 April and the remaining two on 22 April.

On 21 March 1997, Suresh Dewale and Pandurang Durgawali went to the Guhagar police station to lodge a complaint against DPC security guards, who had attacked some buffalo. The officer on duty reportedly refused to accept the complaint unless the complainant changed the description of those accused from the 'company security guards' to 'unknown persons'.

On the evening of 27 February, four goondas (ruffians) came to the house of Adinath Kaljunkar, a leader of the Sangharsh Samiti from Aarey, and threatened to murder him if he continued to oppose the Enron project, as they had taken on-site contracts and would suffer losses. When he telephoned the Guhagar police station, the officer refused to send anyone to investigate. The next morning when he personally went to the police station to file the complaint the officer made a note that the matter had been investigated and was not found to warrant further action—the officer refused to record a complaint.

Police forcibly entered the home of Rajashree and Aparna Dabholkar in Veldur village and dragged them out...three juvenile girls among those detained. Sugandha Vasudev Bhalekar, aged 16, was described as aged 19 on the remand application completed by the police before being placed before the magistrate; similarly Vanita Patekar, aged 15, was described as 20 year of age, and Rekha Padyal, also aged 15 years, was described as a 19 year-old. The raid was conducted early in the morning when most of the men of the village had left to catch fish.

Villagers have also been arrested under section 135 of the Bombay Police Act which provides for imprisonment for up to one year and a fine for those disobeying orders made under section 37 of the Act.

Several of those arrested in connection with these protests have been arrested under section 151 of the Code of Criminal Procedure (CrPC). This section allows police officers to arrest individuals whom they suspect may commit a cognizable offence, without a warrant, and further allows those arrested to be detained for longer than 24 hours by orders of a magistrate. This provision continues to be used notwithstanding the directives of the Bombay High Court, which has held that section 151 should not be used in the guise of maintenance of law and order or to oppress social action groups.

(Between the second week of) February 1997 (and June 1997), nearly 200 villagers have reportedly been issued with undated and unnumbered warning notices under Section 149 of the CrPC accusing them of spreading false information against the government and the company, and warning them that they would be held responsible for any untoward incidents that result in damage to life and property or worsen the law and order situation.

Annexure 1

Letter Dated 21/5/93 from GoM

To GoI

> D.O. No. PSP 1092/CR-2115/NRO-2.
> Industries Energy and Labour Department
> Mantralaya, Bombay - 400 032.
> Date : May 21, 1993

Dear Shri Ramji,

This has reference to your letter dated May 21, 1993 to Shri Nimbalkar, Chairman, Maharashtra State Electricity Board (MSEB) and copy faxed to me today. I understand that the MSEB has already sent its comments to the office of the Secretary (Power) Government of India on 13th May 1993 on a note prepared by the World Bank about the Dabhol Power Project which is an accompaniment to Mr Vergin's letter to Shri Montek Singh Ahluwalia, Secretary, Ministry of Finance, Government of India. Any way I am enclosing views of MSEB again for your reference.

On behalf of the Government of Maharashtra, I would like to add the following points:

(1) The note does not support the Project. It, however, points out very clearly that this project would be a very good project if it was not coming up in India. It also says that its costs compare favourably with the costs of a similar power plant based on imported coal. The World Bank is not satisfied mainly on the ground that the demand does not justify setting up of a large project and that the project would create financial difficulties for MSEB. While the above conclusions appear to be prima facie reasonable, they obviously do not take into account the fact that concomitant with the project is the fact that not merely MSEB would have to improve its grid discipline to absorb the Enron power but it has to improve its general working as well. It may also mean that the tariff structure needs to be much more rational than what it is today.

(2) Possibility of setting up indigenous coal or gas based power stations is not very bright even though the theoretically such an option looks better on economic considerations.

(3) The assessment of the World Bank seems to say that the Enron Project would put a heavy financial burden on MSEB and that the project is not a part of the least cost sequence for power generation in Maharashtra. It is interesting that the World Bank feels that imported coal and not LNG would be a better option for base-load station of MSEB. The enclosed note of Mr Vergin's letter brings out very clearly that the cost of Enron Project compares favourably with the cost of imported coal fired generation unit (para 10, page 3).

(4) The World Bank presumes that the tariff of the LNG based power project from Enron will be very high. It is necessary to carry out the analysis separately, but our belief is that the tariff that MSEB would charge to its consumers would compare favourably with the projected tariff. We are, however, negotiating strongly with Enron Power Corporation and trying to push down the tariff.

(5) In the demand of power, there is a large difference between the day peak and night peak. This problem is accentuated by the adverse thermal hydro mix of the installed capacity in Maharashtra. It is difficult to manage the system during the off peak period. But it is not right to say that there in a large surplus capacity during the off peak hours. In any case,

even the pitmouth coal plants in the State have stocks only for a day or two. Conserving their stocks during the off peak hours will actually enable MSEB to meet the peak demand little more efficiently. Based on our experience, we do not perceive any remarkable change in the coal situation in future. The hydel generation potential of Maharashtra State is in any case limited. Given the background of demand for power registered with the MSEB and the State Government from the industries in Raigad-Ratnagiri region, we are confident that the Enron project can easily run as a base-load station.

We feel confident that Government of India should take up the matter strongly with the World Bank and ask them to review their decision. Their comments may create a problem for the developers to raise commercial and institutional borrowings.

Your sincerely,
(U.K. Mukhopadhyay)
(Secretary)

Shri N. Ramji,
Joint Secretary,
Ministry of Energy,
Department of Power,
Government of India,
Shram Shakti Bhavan,
New Delhi.
Fax No. 11-3717519

Annexure 2

Letter Dated 28/6/93 from Enron to MSEB

ENRON
Development Corp
June 28, 1993

Joseph W. Sutton

Fax: 9122-642-8511

To: Ajit Nimbalkar
From: Joe Sutton
Subject: Dabhol Power Project

Dear Ajit,

I trust this note finds you well. I hope you are having a successful approval process with GoM. I would like to coordinate with you our travel plans and propose a schedule for the next session of negotiations.

I met last week with Linklaters and Freshfields in London. It seems that the PPA has been agreed down to about seven major issues. There are several points that Freshfields will need your approval on but a small number of major issues remain.

Draft 7 (final draft) was fully completed on Monday. Freshfields informed me that they/you would require ten (10) days for review and discussions (5 for you to review in advance and 3-5 days with your team in Bombay) before we could resume our final negotiations. As such, we would like to plan on forming our team on 1 July to resume negotiations. It is our hope that these will take not more than 5 days after which we can sign the PPA.

Chris has informed me that you would like to meet on 8 July. I understand concern with the World Bank Meetings. We agree with the importance of ____ under time constraints and would like to meet sooner if possible. ____ propose beginning, negotiations on 1 July if possible. Let me know your ____

Regardless Rebecca and I will arrive in India early. We plan to ____ members of GoI and hopefully, with the Chief Minister ____ and others in Delhi would be appreciated.

I recently met with the World Bank and have been following the articles in the India papers. I feel that the World Bank opinion can be changed. We will engage a PR firm during the next trip and hopefully manage the media from here on. The project has solid support from all other agencies in Washington. We'll get there! We need now to put the PPA behind us.

As you know, we plan on going to Doha Qatar from Bombay to begin ____ negotiations. We also had good news from Shell in Oman yesterday in London. I don't think LNG will be a problem.

We look forward ____. We have come a long way.

sd —

(Joseph Sutton)

Annexure 3

Note Dated on or Around August 1993 Purporting to be the "Additional Views" of the Finance Department of GoM

Secret

Industries, Energy and Labour Department;
Mantralaya, Bombay - 400 032.

The additional views of Finance Department on the proposal of *Enron regarding setting up Power Project, at Dabhol, District: Ratnagiri* which remained to be incorporated in the Cabinet Note already circulated are as under:

"(1) *Structure of returns*:

(a) Guaranteed returns on capital employed

(b) Precautions against devaluation risk.

Although ENRON Consortium include equipment suppliers and plant erectors viz. General Electric and Bechtel, I am still not sure whether ENRON's share is going to be 255 m. dollars. This is not defined nor the project cost projected has been defined as a ceiling project cost. It is quite possible that in the end, we might end up with cost and time overruns. Secondly, in terms of the agreements that are going to be executed, there does not appear to be any incentive on behalf of the ENRON to curtail the project cost.

The project is primarily based on Liquefied Natural Gas (LNG) which involves very expensive transportation in specially built refrigerated vessels in which the liquefied gas is transported at extremely low temperature. Therefore the cost is going to be very high. LNG input costs have a significant bearing on the final costing of power. It is envisaged that ENRON is to be the sole fund manager but the long term supply contracts are still under negotiation. Unless these are finalised, it would be difficult for us to know exactly what the power is going to cost.

One cannot but feel that the comitment on behalf of the MSEB is open ended in absence of the details mentioned in the preceding paras. Besides, one cannot help feeling that Enron is not taking any risk whatsoever as a generator of power but wants guaranteed rewards which is not a very satisfactory arrangement.

(2) *Funding*:

ENRON has originally committed to raise a large quantum of debt resources through the US EXIM Bank as suppliers of credit. Later, it has approached the World Bank for funding against the sovereign guarantees to be provided by Government of India and it also proposed to procure local resource funding from local financial institutions. In other words, this means that ENRON Project will preempt funds from the World Bank and other institutions to the detriment of other projects of MSEB. In fact, ENRON should have made effort to raise from sources which are not easily accessible to MSEB. Therefore, the approach to the World Bank only serves to erode the available quantum of funding from the Bank for other power projects.

(3) *Weakening the credit structure of the MSEB*:

The project envisages the sale of expensive power to HT industrial users via the MSEB with the profits of such sales being earmarked for payment to ENRON on a preferential basis. Incidentally, this amounts roughly to Rs 250 crore per month. In fact, any special arrangements made for payment of dues to ENRON weakens the residual operations of MSEB, which needs to be serviced by non-HT non-industrial users. This would definitely weaken MSEB and will preclude other MSEB project from being financed.

(4) *Nature of guarantees*:

MSEB guarantees are sought for both purchase of power to the required extent as well as for the LNG tie-up payments. This appears to be not favourable to the MSEB.

The emphasis has all along been on the power purchase agreement, the Central Government having given all the other clearances. To this extent, MSEB has not been in an advantageous position to negotiate the project.

Subject to verification, I heard that ENRON has recently completed a project at Manila and the Government has been embarrassed with a fait accompli. It would be interesting to know what kind of agreement the ENRON had entered into with the Manila Government.

(5) To make the project work, I have the following suggestions to make:

  (i)   ENRON must clearly state the project ceiling cost and finalise the LPG arrangements before we take up the project for discussion.

  (ii) The full set of contractual agreements must be received and finalised, not only the power purchase agreement. This can be done in the light of agreements they may have entered into with the Manila Government.

  (iii) The Western Grid is short of power and, therefore, before we enter into an agreement with ENRON, sharing arrangements for power with the Government of Gujarat and Karnataka needs to be finalised.

  (iv) Lastly, if we enter into an agreement with ENRON without taking adequate precautions, it might lead to serious weakening of financial position of MSEB which will endanger their other projects."

(U.K. Mukhopadhyay)
Secretary (Energy).

Annexure 4

Letter Dated 26/8/93 from ENRON Development Corporation to Government of Maharashtra

ENRON
Development Corp.

Rebecca P. Mark
Chairman President and
Chief Executive Officer

333 Clay Street
Suite - 1600
Houston, Texas - 77002
(713) 646-6010
(713) 646-6161

August 26, 1993
VIA FAX

Mr Sharad Pawar
Honorable Chief Minister
Maharashtra State, Mantralaya
Bombay 400 032, India

Dear Mr Pawar

I understand from our people in Bombay and Delhi that we are making some progress with the Dabhol project approvals. However, it is still not clear when we can expect Cabinet approval and signing of Power Purchase Agreement. A key issue is clearance by CEA. Our people, together with MSEB, have met extensively with CEA this week to answer their questions about the project. The remaining concern seems to reside with Mr Beg, Member Planning for Thermal projects. He continues to hold up project approval based upon the question of demand for power in Maharashtra. No one from the Ministry of Power in Delhi has given direction to Mr Beg to move forward on this issue. Consequently, we have a project under the government's "fast track" program, approved by FIPB, but the CEA refuses to grant a clearance.

The other issues we discussed during our meetings last week were the GoI guarantee for EXIM and the guarantees available to Dabhol Power Corp. for securing LNG purchases. Here is where we are on each of these.

EXIM Guarantee

In our discussions in Delhi, I believe the GoI guarantee of the Power Purchase Agreement is your preferred alternative to a direct guarantee by GoI to US EXIM. We will proceed with a GoI guarantee of the Power Purchase Agreement. We believe we can secure financing from EXIM on this basis. However, we must advise you that under the direct guarantee program, US EXIM can approve the project in 2–3 months and under the scenario you propose with a guarantee of the Power Purchase Agreement, EXIM is expected to take about 12 months for project approval.

Enron, GE and Bechtel will do our best to exert pressure to speed up approval process to that we can complete financing of Phase I as soon as possible. However, the delays in securing financing, when added to the delays we have experienced in getting a commitment from GoM, will cause our schedule for construction of Phase I to slip by several months.

LNG Guarantees

The second issue, of guarantees to Dabhol Power Corp. for LNG supply, has been part of the project from the beginning and is not additional concession. The guarantees were presented as a part of our project during the FIPB approval process. We an agree this issue now or settle the security arrangements for fuel when the LNG contract if farther along. We are willing to proceed by amending Power Purchase Agreement to reflect this as an agreement to be added later.

It is critical that we get the Power Purchase Agreement approved and signed now and that we start Phase I financing immediately. Because of GoM delays in approval and the associated negative press of the last few weeks, the project is in danger. We are working on financing arrangements prior project approval but the banks in India and externally are losing their enthusiasm based on lack of progress. Our letter of intent with Mobil/Qatar expires September will be under no obligation to proceed if there is no cabinet approval by September 31. The delays have also caused us to slip the expected construction start for Phase I from January 1994 to mid-summer 1994 and additional delays will cause further slippage. We need to make immediate progress.

I will work closely with Mr Nimbalkar and Mr Mukhopadhyay to resolve any remaining issues may have. We will also be contracting Mr Verma to schedule a meeting with the FIPB as soon as we have your commitment of the date for review by the Cabinet of Maharashtra. Thank you for your committed support.

Sincerely,
R.P. Mark

Annexure 5

Minutes of Meeting Dated 3/11/93

Confidential

Subject: Minutes of the meeting taken by Finance Secretary on Dabhol Power Project of M/s. Enron Development Corp., USA.

1. Finance Secretary held a meeting at 9.00 a.m. and 5.00 p.m. on 3.11.93 to discuss the tariff for power proposed by M/s. Enron for the above project. A list of those present is attached.

2. Finance Secretary sought clarification on the exact nature of the tariff proposed by the company. The Financial Adviser. MSEB stated that it was not a one part dollar tariff but had been broken down into various cost components. It consisted of two basic parts a capacity charge and an energy charge. The break up of the capacity charge over the period of the Power Purchase Agreement (PPA) as a whole is as under:

   i) 53% of the tariff representing the equity and the dollar debt service component was being escalated at 4% per annum;

   ii) 11% represented dollar O&M charges which was being escalated on the basis of the United States CFI;

   iii) 25% represented taxes and dividend reserve which also escalated at 4% per annum;

   iv) 10% represented the rupee debt service component, which was a pass through item depending on the prevailing interest rates;

   v) 1% was the rupee O&M component.

The energy charge was basically linked to the fuel price and M/s Enron had assumed a 3.5% escalation. This component of the tariff would be determined by actual price of fuel.

3. On the basis of the above calculation, the estimated starting tariff was 7.5 cents per unit in 1997 comprising of 3.89 cents as the capacity charge and 3.61 cents as the energy charge. The charge escalated over time as described above.

4. On the basis of this clarification, it was noted that the tariff was not 100% dollar based but 89% of the capacity charge plus the fuel cost would be dollar linkedimplying an approximate 95% dollar linkage.

5. Finance Secretary sought a clarification on the Internal Rate Return (IRR) to equity assumed in the calculations. The Financial Adviser MSEB stated that the normal IRRR to investors would be 25.22% and assuming an inflation rate of around 3–4%, the real IRR would be 20.6% at 80% availability. Chairman, MSEB stated that in the negotiations they had attempted to bring down this rate but eventually had accepted this figure.

6. The question was raised as to whether this was an unreasonable rate of return. The point was made that a high rate of return could be obtained by keeping down costs and through efficient operations without any adverse effect on the power cost. It was, therefore necessary to consider also the validity of the cost estimates. The Financial Adviser, MSEB stated that they were not competent to comment on capital costs but generally felt that these were not out of line. Chairman, MSEB explained that a comparison had been done with two other projects for which competitive bids had been invited. These projects are based on gas and coal respectively. If the cost of the harbour and storage facilities are excluded since these are additional items the capital costs of the Enron proposal work out to Rs 3.76 crores per MW. Of the short listed bids for the coal/gas projects the bids received showed a capital cost of Rs 3.98 crores per MW. Rs 3.54 crores per MW

respectively. The costs of Enron project were tehrefore not viewed as substantially higher than those received through competitive binding.

7. Having noted that the costs were more or less on par with that of other projects the question of the reasonableness of the IRR was considered M/Power felt that the return was not unreasonable with 90% PLF. MSEB _____ as reasonable based on information received _____ that a 25% IRR would be desirable to attract international investors.

Financial Adviser MSEB stated that their assessment was that domestic investors would require a somewhat lower IRR and of this were to be accepted on optimum blended IRR would be between 17–18.3% in real terms. He clarified that such a reduced IRR could facilitate a negotiation on reduced esclation for capacity charge on the tariff amounting to 0.57 cents/kwh.

Ministry to Power was of the view that the assumption of a lower expected IRR for domestic investors was not consonant with the actual position regarding private sector power projects in India financed by IDBI and confirmed its position regarding the reasonableness of the IRR.

8. The Financial Adviser MSEB also raised the issue of protection of return in foreign currency. He expressed the view taht investment by domestic investors needed to protected only in rupees while that of foreign invetors in dollars. Assuring domestic investors of guaranteed return in dollars in fact added to the tariff since 18–20% of the capacity charge was contributed by domestic equity. He pointed out that foreign equity in these power projects is likely to drop substantially over the years which would burden the tariff with a guaranteed dollar return on higher domestic equity. Finance Secretary observed that Indian Company Law does not allow such differentiation in treatment of investors.

9. A clarification was sought from D/Power regarding the cost of any recently approved power project. It was indicated that the relevant PIB approval would be Gandhar for which orders were placed in 1992 at Rs 3.4 crores per MW based on domestic gas Finance Secretary noted that in general power projects had substantial cost over-runs over the original PIB approved estimates. There was advantage therefore, in a proposal such as that of M/s. Enron where the construction costs and risks were undertaken by the company.

10. The question of fuel cost was also considered. It was noted that the fuel manager appointed by Dabhol Power Corpn. could enter into long term supply contracts but MSEB retained the right to approve cash contract and also arrange for quotations to be submitted to the fuel manager. Discussions between M/s. Enron and MSEB had been held and various formulations considered based on the Platt index. It was also recognised that distillates are an internationally traded commodity and it would be possible to ensure that a competitive price was being obtained.

11. Finance Secretary enquired regarding the tariff in the Hub River project of Pakistan. Financial Adviser MSEB stated that in the Hub River Project, there was frcnt loading of tariff which declined gradually over the years. The annualised tariff would be 5.9 cents per unit. By way of comparison after excluding import duties and corporate taxes and removing the inflation element, the annualised tariff for Enron would be around 5.71 cents per unit while that for Hub Valley would be 5.4 cents per unit at 75% PLF including 10% import duties. This is arising because of the lower IRR of the Hub river project.

12. The Financial Adviser pointed out that the protection in dollar afforded to domestic investors would expose the SEBs to additional foreign exchange risk he suggested that it may be possible to work out a system whereby the domestic investors are protected in rupee terms. He proposed that an agreement could be arrived at between SEBs and the foreign investors through a management system of other direct arrangements whereby separate payments would be made to cover the foreign exchange and element for the investors. He felt that this was an important issue since the decision on M/s. Enron would determine the pattern for various other foreign investment proposal in the pipeline. His discussions with Ms Enron indicated that they would be prepared to accept this position.

13. The making took note of the positive features of the project:
  i) relatively early availability of power;
  ii) high plant load factor;
  iii) favourable psychological impact for foreign investment in the power sector;
  iv) an alternative fuel source for Maharashtra;
  v) a fixed tariff with risk being borne by the company.

(Dinkar Khullar)
8.11.93

FINANCE SECRETARY
SECRETARY, POWER
CHIEF SECRETARY, MAHARASHTRA

PRESENT

MINISTRY OF FINANCE
  1. Finance Secretary
  2. Secretary, Revenue
  3. Chief Economic Adviser
  4. Deputy Secretary (Shri M. Prasad) CEA

MINISTRY OF POWER
  5. Secretary, Power
  6. Special Secretary
  7. FA (Shri Sethumadhavan)
  8. Director (Shri A.K. Upadhyaya)

MAHARASHTRA GOVERNMENT
  9. Chairman, MSEB
  10. Financial Adviser MSEB (Sh. R. Mathrani)
  11. Chief Engineer (Sh. Harnay)

PMO
Dt. Secy. (Ms Manjula Subramaniam)
Director (Sh. Dinkar Khullar)

TELEPHONE (O) 602083

Annexure 6

Minutes of FIPB Meeting Dated 10/11/93

Confidential

PRIME MINISTER'S OFFICE

PMO D.O. No. 740/34/C/01/93-EWS   Dated
10.11.93

Summary Record of the Foreign Investment Promotion Board (FIPB) Meeting Held on 5.11.93

Proposal of M/s. ENRON:

1. The representatives of M/s ENRON met the Board to seek clarifications on policy issues relating to the project.

2. Finance Secretary observed that the question of cost of power had been looked into and it had been found that it was more or less in line with other projects being put up in Maharashtra. The only area of some concern remained the question of the exchange protection on return being afforded to domestic equity. This was originally intended only to reassure the foreign investors. He asked the representatives of M/s ENRON whether any formulation could be evolved to tackle this issue within the framework of Company law under which no differentiation could be made in rates of dividends for foreign and domestic investors. M/s ENRON indicated hat they had examined this matter in depth and considered various options. Within the frame work of Company Law, no practical solution had emerged. While they were sympathetic regarding the problem, they felt that any attempted situation would expose them to problems either of taxes or legal interpretation. The Board noted that this remained something of a problem but no immediate solution could be found and there was scope for further discussions on this issue. On the specific policy matters, the following was indicated:

I. GoI Counter Guarantee

The Board explained that they would be in a position to recommend the idea of the counter guarantee to the CCFI. As regards the legal document to be finalised, this may require discussions and M/s ENRON was requested to leave behind a member of their team for discussions on the subject to finalise the text of the Agreement which would be coordinated by Secretary Power.

II. Foreign Currency Bank Account

Finance Secretary had already indicated, in principle, approval subject to the condition that the accounts would be used for meeting specific foreign exchange expenses and not for holding the working balances of the Company. Reconversion to defray rupee expenditure would not be part of the provisions. These details would be worked out with RBI.

III. 5-Year Tax Holiday for Phase II

The Board indicated that in principle, this could not be considered for phase II of the project should it be taken up. The matter will be processed for approval of the appropriate authorities. Secretary (Revenue) indicated that on the other tax related issues there should be no problem.

IV. CEA Clearance

Secretary, Power indicated that this clearance should be available in the work beginning 8th November, 1993.

3. In separate discussions, Secretary, Petroleum had confirmed that, as a special case, the company would be allowed to import fuel for this project subject to its not using infrastructure facilities of the public sector _____ and existing port infrastructure. (The reference to the subject in the Summary Record of Discussion of the FIPB Meeting of 16.10.1993 stands appropriately modified.)

4. The Board assured M/s ENRON that the matters for approval will be expeditiously taken up. Note had been taken of the target date for approvals proposed by M/s ENRON.

(Dinkar Khullar)
Director

Cabinet Secretary
Finance Secretary
Foreign Secretary
Secretary, Industrial Development
Commerce Secretary
Secretary, Revenue
Secretary, Power
Secretary, Petroleum
Chief Secretary, Maharashtra

ATTENDANCE
1. Principal Secretary (in chair)
2. Principal Secretary
3. Commerce Secretary
4. Secretary, Power
5. Secretary, Revenue
6. Additional Secretary (—) MEA (Shri P.M.S. Malik)
7. Additional Secretary Dept. of ID (Shri P.G. Mankad)
8. JS (S), PMO
9. Director (K), PMO

GOVT. OF MAHARASHTRA
1. Chief Secretary
2. Chairman MSEB
3. Financial Adviser, MSE
4. Chief Engineer, MSEB

Annexure 7

Government of India
Secretary

Ministry of Power
Shram Shakti Bhawan,
Rafi Marg, New Delhi - 110 001

D.O. No. C-91/93-IPC (Vol.)   11th November '93.

Dear Shri Gambhir,

With reference to our telephone talk, I quote the extracts from the minutes of FIPB meeting held on 5.11.93:

"Finance Secretary observed that the question of cost of power had been looked into it had been found that it was more or less in line with other Maharashtra."

With regards,

Your sincerely,
(R. Vasudevan)

Shri Y.P. Gambhir,
Chairman, CEA
New Delhi.

Annexure 8

Minutes of 118th Meeting of the Central Electricity Authority on 12/11/93

Summary record of discussions of the 118th Meeting of Central Electricity Authority or Techno-Economic Appraisal of Power development schemes.
First session held on 12.11.93 at 3.00 p.m.
Second session held on 16.11.93 at 3.00 p.m.

FIRST SESSION

List of participants is at Annex-I

Item 1: Dabhol CCGT Plant - 2015 MW (net) in Maharashtra by M/s. Dabhol Power Company Ltd. (of M/s. Enron, USA) Estimated Completion Cost: US $2828.524 milliion = Rs 9051.27 crores.

1.1 Introducing the scheme, Chief Engineer (TPA) stated aht the proposal was for setting up of an LNG based Combined Cycle Gas Turbine (CCGT) Plant of 2015 MW (net) capacity by M/s Dabhol Power Company (IPC) of M/s Enron, USA. The following brief details of the scheme were presented:

Phase-I	695 MW (net) capacity to the fuelled by imported distillate fuel till commissioning of Phase-II
Phase-II	1320 MW (net) capacity to be fuelled imported Liquified Natural Gas (LNG) Total −2015 MW (Phase I & II)
Completion cost (including taxes and duties)	Phase-I (1996) US $ 863.651 million (Rs 2763.68 Crs.) Phase-II (1998) US $ 1964.873 million (Rs 6287.59 Crs.) Total: US $ 2828.524 million (Rs 9051.27 crores)
Sale rate of electricity	Phase-I—US cents 7.47/Kwh (Rs 2.39/Kwh) = 1st year Phase-II—US cents 7.62/Kwh (Rs 2.44/Kwh) = 1st year
Exchange rate 1 US $ = Rs 32.00	
Clerances/ inputs to be tied up	— Sec. 29 of E (S) Act, 1948 — State Govt. approval — Clearance of CWC for water availability — Clearance of Ministry of Environment and Forests for power plant and harbour — Clearance of Port Authority for construction of harbour — Clearance of NNA for stack height
Commissioning schedule	March 1996 for Phase-I July 1997 for Phase-II

1.2 Dy. Adviser, Planning Commission read out the observations of Adviser (Energy), Planning Commission. His observations were:

   i) From sustem operation point of view it would perhaps be advantageous to consider or setting up of pumped storage schemes in the Western region. The implications of the likely power exchange between the Southern and Western regions through the proposed HVDC would have to be kept in view while considering the new capacity additions.

   ii) The backing down of the existing thermal generation capacity in Maharashtra due to this new capacity addition would imply heavy additional economic costs imposed on the power system of MSEB and these costs needed to be quantified and net economic rate of return from Dabhol project computed.

   iii) Keeping in view the costliest option of distillate fuel/LNG, the difference between the cost of LNG based power and the least cost option for Dabhol should be quantified.

   iv) Any addition to generation capacity should be meatched by corresponding investment on T&D works, the present allocation for T&D works being only 27.7% of the power sector outlay of Maharashtra.

   v) The objective should be to minimize the cost of supply of electricity to the consumers in Maharashtra in the context of prevailing low electricity tariff structure in various states including Western region.

He concluded with the remark that CEA should consider these aspects before taking a final view on the proposal.

1.3 It was noted that Dabhol CCGT was to be set up in private sector for meeting power requirements of Maharashtra. As per studies carried out by the Planning Wing of CEA, power from Phase-I (695 MW) could be absorbed by Maharashtra System. However, the state would be surplus both in capacity and energy for three years with commissioning of Phase-II of the project in 1997–98. Therefore, to ensure full utilisation of power from the project including off-peak energy, Maharashtra authorities would have to enter into firm commercial agreements with other states within and/or outside the region through the existing inter-regional HVDC link between the Northern and Western Regions and recently sanctioned HVDC link between Western and Southern regions. In the absence of firm commercial arrangements to ensure absorptions of power as mentioned above, MSEB would have to postpone the commissioning of Phase-II of the project. Director (IPC), MoP stated taht as per Power Purchase Agreement, under negotiation between Maharashtra authorities and M/s Enron, there was no commitment on the part of Govt. of Maharashtra for Phase II of the project and it could be postponed or even abandoned.

1.4 Chairman observed that since the project was scheduled for commissioning in a short time of about 2–3 years (by March 1996 and July, 1997), MSEB would have to ensure that the transmission scheme would be completed in time to match with commissioning programme of generation scheme.

Chief Engineer (PSP) stated that proposals for associated transmission system had been received from MSEB and if Phase II was uncertain, the transmission scheme would have to be reviewed by MSEB, Member (G&O) observed that telemetering arrangement, should be available both at the Power Plant and associated transmission system and the cost involved would not be high. CE (PSP) clarified that in so far as the associated transmission scheme was concerned, this has been taken care of in the scheme submitted by MSEB.

1.5 It was observed that as per the studies conducted by CEA, Dabhol CCGT plant was not the least cost option. CE (TPA) stated that MSEB had other less costly options such as Kaparkheda Unite 3 and 4 (2 × 210 MW), Kaparkheda-Unite 5 and 6 (2 × 250 MW), Umred TPS-1000 MW, but these scheme were in the preliminary stages. Member (HE) pointed out that these projects being in preliminary stages, could not be considered for comparision purposes as they would not be available for meeting the power demand in the same time frame.

1.6   CE (TPA) stated that fuel for Phase-I of the project would be light distillate No. 2 import origin and after completion of Phase-II, LNG from Qatar for the whole Plant. In regard to LNG fuel for power generation, Ministry of Power was earlier informed that LNG could not be least cost option. The project proposal of M/s DPC was, however, essentially based on imported LNG.

1.7   CE (TPA) stated that the tariff for sale of power from the project was not as per GoI notification dated 30th March, 1992. He further stated hat in response to request for details of cost estimates, M/s DPC informed in a letter dated 10.11.93 that the capital cost of the project was irrelevant to CEA because the tariff was guaranteed and changes in capital cost were not passed on to the customer in the tariff. Chairman observed that the Dabhol tariff was a negotiated one and a communication was received from the Ministry of Power informing that the cost of power had been looked into by the Ministry of Finance and found to be more or less in line with other projects being put up in Maharashtra. As such, tariff aspects and deviations with reference to GoI notification and cost estimates could not be examined in the CEA.

1.8   CE (Commercial) stated that the tariff proposed was a negotiated one and not as per GoI notification or related to the capital cost and payments involved foreign exchange outgo. The return on equity would work out to about 26% in the 5th year increasing to 52% during the 15th year if the tariff of M/s DPC was adopted for calculations. Exemptions for deviations from GoI tariff notification including return on equity and other aspects would need to be looked into by the Ministry of Power and other concerned agencies of GoI.

1.9   Member (P) observed that as the World Bank had not agreed to finance the project there would be a gap of US $ 600 million in the financing plan indicated by M/s DPC. Director (IPC), MOP replied that M/s Enron were no longer seeking World Bank financing and would be arranging the funds from other sources.

(Chairman stated that in view of the replies received from M/s DPC in regard to cost estimates, clarification by the Ministry of Power on financial package and the examination of tariff aspects by Ministry of Finance, examination by CEA would, in effect get limited to the technical aspects and need for the project, which was already discussed.) Chief Engineer (C) expressed the view that given this background, the completed cost would not be considered by CEA at a later stage.

1.10   Member (PS) stated that since the tariff was designated in dolar terms, MSEB should absorb the associated exchange rate variations as other states purchasing the power may not agree to pay in foreign exchange or absorb variations in foreign exchange. Further, since the fuel supply would be from Qatar, in the event of any political problems, fuel supply might not be available and MSEB might not be able to meet its commitments to the consumers. In such an event, M/s DPC should compensate MSEB. Chairman stated that the aspects relating to import and security of imported fuel supplies, foreign exchange outgo, etc. would need to be considered by the appropriate agencies/authorities in the Government of India.

1.11   Member (E & C) observed that in absence of compliance with Section 29 of E (S) Act, 1948, by the project authorities, formal clearance to the scheme could not be accorded. Chief Engineer, CWC, pointed out that the consent of state revenue authorities for land availability for the project was awaited. This aspect would have to be taken care of by the state authorities.

1.12   After discussions, it was decided that the Ministry of Power might be informed that in view of the fact that (i) the tariff for power from the project was negotiated one and not in conformity with GoI notification, and not related to the capital cost and (ii) cost of power from the project had been looked into by the Ministry of Finance, only the technical aspects of the scheme were examined in CEA and found to be generally in order. Formal communication of clearance to technical aspects of the scheme could be given after compliance of Section 29 of the E(S) Act, 1948 by M/s DPC subject to the following conditions:

i)   State Govt.'s approval to M/s DPC to establish, operate and maintain the power plant;

ii)   Clearance of Ministry of Environment and Forests for power plant and harbour/port;

iii) Clearance of port authorities for construction of the harbour/ port;
iv) Clearance of National Airport Authority for stack height 98m;
v) Clearance of Central Water Comm. for water availability;
vi) Before starting Phase II of the project, Maharashtra Govt./ MSEB will ensure that the entire power from the project including off-peak surplus will be absorbed within the Maharashtra system or if necessary by entering into agreement with entities outside Maharashtra.
vii) MSEB will ensure completion of associated transmission system matching with the commissioning schedule of the project.

The aspects relating to import of fuel, foreign exchange outgo and deviations from GoI tariff notifications including return on equity may be looked into by the Ministry of Power and other concerned agencies in the GoI.

List of Participants

118th CEA meeting held on 12.11.93 (First Section)
Shri Y.P. Gambhir, Chairman, CEA......in Chair

CENTRAL ELECTRICITY AUTHORITY
Shri M.I. Beg, Member (P)
Shri H.C. Mital, Member (PS)
Shri S.R. Narasimhan, Member (HE)
Shri M.P. Ramanan, Member (T)
Shri B. Sengupta, Member (G&O)
Shri S.N. Shende, Member (E&C)
Shri V.V.R.K. Rao, Secretary, CEA

MINISTRY OF POWER
Shri N. Ramji, JS (IPC)

PLANNING COMMISSION
Shri L.P. Sonkar, Dy. Adviser (Power)
Shri D.S. Arora, Dy. Adviser (Power)

CENTRAL WATER COMMISSION
Shri T. Subba Rao, CE (HP)

CENTRAL ELECTRICITY AUTHORITY
Shri K.N. Sinha, CE (Commercial)
Shri Rajendra Singh, CE (HEP)
Shri B.K. Gaur, CE (HPA)
Shri S. Sethvandatham, CE (TPA)
Shri K. Ramanathan, CE (PSP)
Shri S.L.N. Prabhu, CE (pl-I)
Shri Arun Sarkar, CE (Chairman's Office)
Shri K.V.K. Prema Kumar, Director (PAC)
Shri R. Srinivasan, Director (TPIA II)
Shri R.S. Chadha, Director (HPA I)
Shri S.S. Jolly, DD (PAC)

Annexure 9

Maharashtra State Electricity Board (Tentative Tariff Projections for Dabhol Project with Customs Duty on Project Equipment and Fuel)

Assumptions:

(1) Exchange Rate as per the table indicated by World Bank
(2) Escalation of capacity charge: 4.0% per annum
(3) 100% US $ determined capacity charge
(4) Oil price CIF 4.51 $/MMBTU
(5) Gas prices CIF 3.80 $/MMBTU in 1998
(6) Escalations on oil & gas price: 3.5% per annum

Year:	1993	1994	1995
Rs per $	32.8	34.8	36.9

Year	OIL 1996	1997	GAS 1998	1999	2000	2001	2002	2003	2004	2005	2006	2007	2008	2009	2010	2011	2012	2013	2014
Exchange rate	38.9	40.0	41.2	42.8	43.1	43.5	43.8	44	44.3	44.5	44.7	44.9	45	45.2	45.3	45.4	45.5	45.7	45.8
Capacity charge cents/kwh	3.99	4.15	4.39	4.57	4.75	4.94	5.14	5.34	5.55	5.78	6.01	6.25	6.50	6.76	7.03	7.31	7.60	7.91	8.22
Rs/kwh	1.55	1.65	1.81	1.92	2.03	2.23	2.34	2.44	2.44	2.55	2.67	2.79	2.92	3.04	3.18	3.31	3.45	3.80	3.75
Energy charge cents/kwh	3.95	4.09	3.43	3.55	3.67	3.80	3.94	4.07	4.22	4.35	4.52	4.67	4.84	5.01	5.18	5.38	5.55	5.75	5.95
Rs/kwh	1.54	1.64	1.41	1.49	1.57	1.64	1.71	1.78	1.85	1.93	2.01	2.03	2.17	2.25	2.24	2.43	2.52	2.61	2.72
Total Tariff cents/kwh	7.94	8.28	7.82	8.12	8.42	8.74	9.07	9.41	9.71	10.1	10.5	10.9	11.3	11.7	12.2	12.6	13.1	13.8	14.1
Rs/kwh	3.09	3.30	3.22	3.41	3.60	3.77	3.95	4.12	4.30	4.43	4.59	4.93	5.09	5.29	5.52	5.74	5.97	6.21	8.74

Assumptions:
(1) Exchange Rate as per the table indicated by West Merchant Bank
(2) Escalation of capacity charge: 4.0% per annum
(3) 100% US $ determined capacity charge
(4) Oil price CIF 4.51 $/MMBTU
(5) Gas prices CIF 3.80 $/MMBTU in 1998
(6) Escalations on oil & gas price: 3.5% per annum

Year:	1993-94	1994-95	thereafter
Devaluation:	15%	12%	7%

Year	OIL 1996	1997	GAS 1998	1999	2000	2001	2002	2003	2004	2005	2006	2007	2008	2009	2010	2011	2012	2013	2014
Exchange rate	44.10	47.20	50.50	54.02	57.31	61.85	65.8	70.81	75.77	81.10	85.5	92.82	99.82	106.2	113.7	121.8	130.1	139.8	147.8
Capacity charge cents/kwh	3.99	4.15	4.39	4.57	4.75	4.94	5.14	5.34	5.55	5.78	6.01	6.25	6.50	6.76	7.03	7.31	7.60	7.91	8.22
Rs/kwh	1.75	1.95	2.22	2.47	2.74	3.05	3.10	3.78	4.21	4.65	5.13	5.80	6.45	7.13	8.39	8.85	9.90	11.9	12.08
Energy charge cents/kwh	3.95	4.09	3.43	3.55	3.67	3.80	3.94	4.07	4.22	4.35	4.52	4.67	4.84	5.01	5.18	5.38	5.55	5.75	5.95
Rs/kwh	1.74	1.93	1.73	1.92	2.12	2.35	2.63	2.88	3.19	3.54	3.86	4.34	4.85	5.32	5.85	6.55	7.22	8.30	8.79
Total Tariff cents/kwh	7.94	8.28	7.82	8.12	8.42	8.74	9.07	9.41	9.71	10.1	10.5	10.9	11.3	11.7	12.2	12.6	13.1	13.8	14.1
Rs/kwh	3.50	3.89	3.95	4.34	4.87	5.41	6.00	6.87	7.40	8.22	9.18	10.14	11.25	12.5	13.89	15.42	17.13	19.62	21.12

Annexure 10

Letter Dated 23/11/93 from the GOM to the CEA

CPSP 1093/CR 2230/NR-42
Industries, Energy and Labour Department
Maharashtra Mantralaya, Bombay - 400 032
Date: 23 November 1993

To,

The Chairman,
Central Electricity Authority
New Delhi.
Fax No. 6877267   Attn: Shri Gambhir

Sir,

Please find enclosed a letter from M/s. Enron in which they have said that they have not received any objections pursuant to the publication of the Notification about the proposed Dabhol Powr Project. It would, therefore, appear that the requirements of Section 29 of the Electricity (Supply) Act have been met.

Yours faithfully,
(U.K. Mukhopadhyay)
Secretary of Government

Copy to:
Shri N. Ramji,
Joint Secretary, Ministry of Energy,
Government of India,
New Delhi - 110 001
Fax No. - 11-3717519
Chairman, MSEB, Bombay.

Annexure 11

"Clearance" Dated 26/11/93 of the CEA to the DPC

Central Electricity Authority
Sewa Bhavan, R.K. Puram,
New Delhi - 110 066

No. 2/MHA/20/93-PAC/

26th November, 1993

M/s Dabhol Development Corp.
P.O. Box - 1188,
Houston, Texas - 77251-1188
USA.

Subject: Dabhol CCGT Plant - 2015 MW (net) in Maharashtra by M/s Dabhol Power Company Limited (of M/s Enron, USA)

Estimated Completion Cost: US $ 2828.524 million (Rs 9051.27 crores)

Sir,

The above proposal of M/s Dabhol Power Company Limited was considered by the CEA in 118th CEA meeting held on 12th November, 1993. The technical aspects of the scheme hav ebeen accorded clearance of the CEA subject to the following conditions:

i) State Govt's approval to M/s DPC to establish, operate and maintain the power plant.

ii) Clearance of MOEF—for power plant and harbour/port.

iii) Clearance of port authorities for construction of the harbour/port.

iv) Clearance of NAA for stack height of 98m.

v) Clearance of CWC for water availability.

vi) Before starting Phase-II of the project, Maharashtra Govt./ MSEB will ensure that the entire power from the project including off peak surpluses will be absorbed within the Maharashtra system or if necessary by entering into agreements with entities outside Maharashtra.

vii) MSEB will ensure completion of associated transmission system matching with the commissioning schedule of the project.

The aspect relating to import of fuel, foreign exchange outgo and deviation from Government of India's tariff notification including return on equity have been examined by FIPB and the project has been found acceptable by them.

Yours faithfully,
(V.V.R.K. Rao)
Secretary, CEA

Annexure 12

Phone: 6443578/6422211
Telex: 011-78293/78294
Gms: GENGRID
Fax: 91 22 6401329

Corporate Planning Sec.
Prakashgad, 3rd Floor
Bandra (East)
Bombay - 400 051

REF no.: CP/DPC/845

Date: September 30, 1994

To,

The Secretary (Energy)
Govt. of Maharashtra
Mantralaya, Bombay - 400 032

Sub: Tariff Structure: Dabhol Powr Project

Ref.:

1. Secretary, Central Electricity Authority's letter no. 2/Mah/20/ 93-PAC/2862-64 dt. 20th September 1993, addressed to Dabhol Power Company, with a copy to your office with a copy to Chairman, MSEB.

2. Secretary, Central Electricity Authority's letter no. 2/Mah/20/ 94-PAC/1097-1101 dt. 14th July 1994, addressed to Dabhol Power Company, with a copy to your office and Chairman, MSEB.

3. Your letter no. PSP/1037/2115/Vol. 4/NRG-2 dt. 8th Dec. 93 addressed to Dabhol Power Company with a copy to Chairman MSEB.

4. OSD (Tariff), Ministry of Energy, Deptt. of Power, Govt. of India, New Delhi's letter no. 6/1/PTH/93-94 dt. 28th Aug. 94 alongwith Govt., of India's tariff Notification No. SO/605(e) dt. 22nd August 94.

5. Your office letter No. PSP/1094/CR7115 dt. 15/9/94 alongwith Jt. Secretary (IPC)'s D.O. letter No. C.912/94. IPC dt. 8/9/94.

A) This is to state that Maharashtra State Electricity Board had already examined the tariff structure of the Dabhol Power Company and accordingly intimated the Central Electricity Authority, vide MSEB's letter No. CH/ND/ARJ/ENRON/252 dt. 17/9/93 (copy enclosed for reference) that the tariff offered by M/s. Enron is lower than that calculated on the basis of wo-part tariff notified by Govt. of India. CEA had also mentioned the above in their letter conveying their in-principle clearance (reference 2 above). The following table (1) indicates a comparison of two part tariff and Dabhol tariff (as per the terms of P.P.A. for 695 MW Phase I with customs duty and with a fuel cost escalating at the rate of 3.5% per annum. The assumptions are enclosed herewith.

Year	Notification Tariff (Rs/kwh)	DPC Tariff (Rs/kwh)
1997	2.85	2.40
1998	2.88	2.50
1999	2.91	2.60

2000	2.94	2.70
2001	2.98	2.81
2002	3.02	2.92
2003	3.07	3.03
2004	3.13	3.07
2005	3.27	3.14
2006	3.51	3.24
2007	3.78	3.25
2008	3.50	3.35
2009	3.51	3.46
2010	3.66	3.59
2011	3.81	3.71
2012	3.96	3.85
2013	4.12	3.99
2014	4.28	4.14
2015	4.46	4.30
2016	4.65	4.47

The above table demonstrates that the overall per unit tariff calculated on the basis of the norms set out to the PPA is lower than the overall per unit tariff calculated on the basis of the norms specified in the notification.

Annexure 13

Letter Dated 23/12/94 from the CEA to the GOI

Government of India
Central Electricity Authority
Sewa Bhawan, R.K. Puram
New Delhi - 110 066

No. 1-3(13)/94-Secy
23 December, 1994

Shri Pradip Baijal,
Joint Secretary (IPC),
Ministry of Power,
New Delhi

Subject: M/s Dabhol Power Company

Sir,

This has reference to our letter of even number dated 22 December, 1994 and the telephone conversation between SS(P) and Chairman, CEA on the subject. The matter has been further discussed by CEA.

As you are aware, the cost of power has been found to be reasonable by the Ministry of Finance, CEA feels that since the cost of power is to be derived from the capital cost, the Capital cost of Dabhol project may also considered to be reasonable.

Thanking you,

(R.B. Mathur)
Secretary, CEA

Copy to Special Secretary (Power)

Annexure 14

Statement on Enron by L.K. Advani, Bharatiya Janta Party, July 1997

The Maharashtra Government's decision to scrap the Enron deal is the first step against the prevailing culture of corruption in high places. The phenomenon of "foot-through liberalisation", seems to have reached a peak point in this deal, an accord reached in vulgar haste and in unprecedented secrecy the reign of the previous Congress regime in Maharashtra. Apologists for Enron, as for instance former Chief Minister Shri Sharad Pawar, have denounced this as a political decision. If they mean thereby petty poll considerations, they are totally off the mark. The decision is essentially in discharge of the mandate received by the State Government. But these detractors of ours are right in one sense. The decision to scrap the Enron deal is propped not just by economic wisdom. It isindeed a political decision against the political corruption. It is protest against the Swiss bank account culture of Bofors and the suitcase practices of Bombay brokers, which have brought Indian politics disrepute.

Enron's own officers admitted that the corporation spent a little over Rs 62 crores a figure in the same heavyweight category as Bofors in "educating" Indians. The country would certainly like to discover the names of the politicians and officials who thus "graduated" from the Enron School of Business. It would be in place to mention some broad facts about the deal if only to dispel the disinformation being spread in its regard. First: the Shiv-Sena— BJP did not attack the Enron deal to gain any partisan image. The list of those who fought Enron is a long one, cutting across the political spectrum. I would like to mention some: Sudhakar Rao Naik, former Chief Minister of Maharashtra. Enron first appeared during his time. On the pertinent file he wrotel, "An independent study by energy economist should precede any negotiation". The Pawar government ignored this altogether. Second: The World Bank M.S.E.B. approached it to judge technical viability, Enron sought from the World Bank financial assistance. Both were rebuffed, the World Bank affirmed that the project was not viable. The World Bank described the MOU signed with Enron as "one-sided". Third: The Finance Secreatary of Maharashtra, Shri Padmanabhiah, now the Home Secretary of India, fought the deal at every stage. He was over-ruled by his political bosses. Fourth: The Parliamentary Standing Committee on Energy has unanimaously criticised the deal. Fifth, The Planning Commission of India, whose policy paper on energy will show how, wrong the deal. Sixth, in an article published yesterday in the Business Standard, Shri Jairam Ramesh, Adviser to the Planning Commission and part of the Congress Party's own Think ank recalls how he had pleaded strongly with his colleagues in the PMO and Planning Commission to reject Enron's proposal because it was not in national interest. What is even more significant is his observation that his view was supported by no less a person than Finance Minister Shri Manmohan Singh! None of those named above fought for political reasons. Each did so because the deal was against sound economic priciples. Little wonder, therefore, that the Maharashtra Government's decision has been widely acclaimed. Support to the scraping of Enron cuts across party lines. No other recent development has receive such effusive plaudits as this one.

There is yet another reason for these warm kudos, apart from the bad economics of the deal. The entire country feels proud that the Maharashtra Government firmly stood up to arm twisting and pressurising by either power giants or giant powers. By this one single decision, the Shiv-Sena—BJP Government of Maharashtra has made it clear to all concerned that it has no objection to foreign investment in the power sector, it is not prepared to suffer any abridgement of the nations economic sovereignty. Foreign investment are welcome but on terms mutually advantageous, and certainly not one-sided as was this Enron deal.

I would also like to highlight a disturbing, but tall-tale aspect of the deal. First, the indecent haste shown in activating the contract. After MSEB and Enron signed the deal in June, 1993, it lay dormant for 20 month until 25 February, 1995. On that day the Government of Maharashtra suddenly decided to give the go-ahead. The significance of 25 February was that it was one of those days when voting for the Assembly was over, but counting had not yet begun Exit polls, however, had correctly predicted a Congress debacle. Thus, it was a decision taken by a lameduck ministry. Indecent haste is, at best, culpable incompetence. At worst, it is criminal acquiescence. By its own admission the Dabhol project is the costliest of any that Enron had built anywhere in the world. Incidentally, the cheapest also came up in Asia namely, China. In other projects the price of power called for showing down as time passes in Enron's graph the prices kept zooming skyward. These are facts available with the Union Ministry of Energy. The records will also demonstrate that Enron had incorrect data at least twice to MSEB. They provided wrong figures for the cost of a project in Britain. Second, Enron did not disclose that it is the largest producer of natural gas. At no point did MSEB/Maharashtra Government/Government of India contest Enron's figures, its choice of site, or other decision, let above consider another partner. It was Enron, and Enron alone commercial ideology accompanied by an utter lack of transparency. It was possible this lack of openness led to the BJP's poll pledge to re-estimate the Enron Project. The standby which was soon revealed. Enron's misleading statements, MSEB's unconditional surrender, and the remarkable speed with which the project was approved on 25 February, 1995 lead to one conclusion. The numerous economic studies had already dismissed the Dabhol project as milestone around the neck of Maharashtra's citizens, or thanks to prescribe counter guarantees, of India herself. It is significant that the National Working group on Power comprising experts in the power fields has in a statement yesterday welcomed the Maharashtra Governments decision, criticized the Government of India's approach to the patterns in this sector and warned that if New Delhi's attitude remains what it is, there would be a source power famine in the country soon. The NWGP has strongly endorsed the recommendation of Parliaments Standing committee on Power that GoI's current power policy be thoroughly revised.

The BJP believes that India is on the threshold of an industrial revolution. We need cheap power to enable our enterprises to compete on the global level. Projects as burdensome and costly as Enron's will reverse this progress. The BJP also believes that India own hydropower resources have not yet been trapped. Nor have we utilised our coal resources. Third, depending upon power plants that require imported fuel is more than poor economics and commercialization it is also a strategic risk. Fourth, and most important, BJP believes that sweet heart clients like Enron struck in a hush—hush manner are incorrect. Scrapping it is a first step to cleaner politics. We welcome any company that offers power. However, we shall stand firm against companies that dabble in power politics. In the article referred to earlier Shri Jairam Ramesh Advisor to the Planning Commission observes, "The power sector (today) is in a mess, We now have a historic opportunity to clean up the mess. The Unfortunate Enron episode would have served a useful purpose if it forces us to go back to basics."

Index